Rebel Without a Pause

Rebel Without a Pause

A Memoir

Nick Ternette

Foreword by Lawrie Cherniack

Roseway Publishing
an imprint of Fernwood Publishing
Halifax & Winnipeg

Photos: pg. 5, Stan Rossowski; pgs. 60, 109, Paul Graham; pg. 65,
Glenn Michalchuk; pgs. 113, 153 QMI Agency, all reprinted with permission.
All other photos courtesey of Nick and Emily Ternette.

Editing: Sandra McIntyre and Jessica Antony
Text design: Brenda Conroy
Cover design: John van der Woude
Printed and bound in Canada

Published in Canada by Roseway Publishing
an imprint of Fernwood Publishing
32 Oceanvista Lane, Black Point, Nova Scotia, B0J 1B0
and 748 Broadway Avenue, Winnipeg, Manitoba, R3G 0X3
www.fernwoodpublishing.ca/roseway

Fernwood Publishing Company Limited gratefully acknowledges the financial support of
the Government of Canada through the Canada Book Fund, the Canada Council for the
Arts, the Nova Scotia Department of Tourism and Culture and the Province of Manitoba,
through the Book Publishing Tax Credit, for our publishing program.

Library and Archives Canada Cataloguing in Publication

Ternette, Nick, 1945-2013, author
Rebel without a pause / Nick Ternette; foreword by Lawrie Cherniack.

Includes bibliographical references.
ISBN 978-1-55266-572-5 (pbk.)

1. Ternette, Nick, 1945-2013. 2. Ternette, Nick, 1945-2013—Political activity—
Manitoba—Winnipeg. 3. Political participation—Manitoba—Winnipeg. 4. Political
activists—Manitoba—Winnipeg—Biography. 5. Winnipeg (Man.)—Politics and
government. I. Title.

FC3396.26.T47A3 2013   971.27'4303092   C2013-905833-8

Contents

Foreword
By Lawrie Cherniack

This was not supposed to be a eulogy. Nick was supposed to live to see the publication of this book. Well, his body might be gone, but this book preserves his spirit.

Nick was a character. Oblivious to his surroundings and himself, with no discernible sense of humour, focused always on issues, Nick was different and unforgettable.

But Nick was also character himself. He was completely transparent. What you saw was what you got. Behind the loud voice and his small personal space bubble that always put him too close to you, Nick was an honest and compassionate and dedicated man.

Although he did important work in Calgary for five years in the early 1980s, Nick was a political fixture in Winnipeg — participating in innumerable demonstrations for peace and justice and the issues of the day, challenging unjust human rights, anti-panhandling and anti-freedom-of-speech laws, running for public office, appearing on radio and television as a political commentator and writing political analysis in the form of letters and opinion pieces.

He had unlimited energy and spoke uncompromisingly. Everyone in Winnipeg heard about Nick, not the least because people in power attacked him. He was unique and important.

Nick tells the story in this book of how I first met him on the other side of a telephone call in the late summer of 1967. I was coordinating a Free University, and he wanted to put on a course called "Revolution." His voice was so loud that I had to hold the receiver at arm's length.

His course was the most popular course ever offered at the Free University. Mostly young people, many but not all alienated from mainstream society, were attracted by his openness to ideas, his radical perspective, his intensity and his passion.

This book tells Nick's story. I had the privilege of knowing him through most of it. He wore many hats. Under all of them he was his own man. He marched to his own drummer. And people innately trusted him because he was worthy of their trust — he was there when he was needed, he never wavered from the issues, he always did what he said he would do, he always spoke his truth.

This book also tells Nick's story in his own way. It is discursive, tangential, full of informational segues. It's how he talked. He couldn't tell a story straight because he had to make certain that the full context was always understood. Accept this as you read this book, and you'll learn more and, more importantly, you'll understand Nick a lot better.

Nick was an independent socialist with a strong libertarian and ecological perspective. He had a strong analytical background; he was well read in classical and contemporary Marxist writings. He would dedicate himself to any issues and movements he supported, regardless of who was behind them, and make himself completely available to help.

That meant that he often fostered relationships between groups that may not have wanted relationships with each other, and that meant that, although people used his services, he was at times on the margins of the groups he supported. He didn't mind. He never held grudges. He was a workhorse.

His city hall activities have become well known. In that respect he was the ultimate citizen. What must be pointed out is not how often he ran for political office (twenty times, and as many times defeated), but how right he always was. His issues were the correct ones. If his ideas had been implemented, Winnipeg would have been the better for them.

Because he was always available to do any kind of work to help a cause he believed in, he was easy to take for granted. Only when he became less available because of illness did people realize how important he was to their lives.

In all those years of illness, especially the last three following the amputation of both of his legs, he never allowed himself more than five minutes here or there of self-pity. It was always a matter of where he could do the most good, bring his own experience to play. He was so engaged with life.

As a matter of fact, that was another aspect of how easy it was to take him for granted — he was such a life-force that you felt he would always be there.

I said earlier that Nick was completely transparent. One part of him was visible only when you got close, and may not be apparent to those who read this book. That part was love. He did not show love in any of the conventional ways. He didn't know how to hug or show affection, or even to speak of love. But anyone who met him knew that he was all love, that love is what motivated him and gave him the essential courage to go on with his life.

I was Nick's oldest living friend, and he was one of mine. As he relates in this book, Willie Sheard, Kent Gerecke, Werner Goetze, older friends than I, left him too early. Other newer friends took their places. No friend, however, was as significant to him as Emily, whom he loved, and who had the wisdom — and the patience — to live with him and to love him.

I loved him and miss him. All of us who loved him were so happy that before he died he knew this book would be published. If you didn't meet Nick before, you have the opportunity to meet him now.

I can think of nothing more appropriate to say of Nick than this: "Well done, thou good and faithful servant."

Preface
By Emily Ternette

I met Nick in the fall of 1985. He had just moved back from Calgary after five years to live with his aged father. I actually met him in person for the first time at a restaurant called Moscovitz & Moscovitz (now gone) where he was gathering together the crew for his television show, "Crossfire," on Videon community television. When I applied for the volunteer position of "Researcher," my hope was that the experience would lead me into a paid position in television (my dream job).

When I pulled into the parking lot of the restaurant, there stood this man with long, wild-looking hair, pacing back and forth in front of the door. I figured it must be Nick, so I took a deep breath and got out of my car and approached him. He shook my hand vigorously and with a booming voice said, "You must be Emily." Two weeks later Nick called me up and asked me if I liked foreign films. A little confused by the question, I answered yes (although, to be honest, I hadn't seen many!) and he asked me out to see two German films with subtitles. And the rest, as they say, is history.

One thing that I discovered early on about Nick was that he was very shy. It seemed like such a dichotomy. Here was this man with a huge voice who could stand up in front of hundreds of people and give a speech. Yet, he was almost withdrawn when meeting new people or socializing in a group that he was unfamiliar with.

Nick was passionate about the things that he cared about, and he was incredibly focused. However, as I came to learn all too quickly, that passion and focus leant themselves to two main areas — politics and sports — in that order!

I never had any interest in politics. I came from an upper middle-class background where you did your duty and voted the way your parents and grandparents did every four years. To be honest, I found American politics infinitely more interesting than Canadian politics — especially Canadian civic politics, which I found boring! Who would sit for hours listening to

Nick Ternette

people talk about garbage pick-up or snow clearing? And who would want to take the time to make such presentations?

The answer to that, of course, is Nick. Shortly after I met him he ran for mayor in Winnipeg's 1986 election. It was during that campaign that I learned that there were more issues than garbage pick-up and snow clearing. Nick made fervent and eloquent speeches about people living in poverty in Winnipeg, the homeless, our "broken" bus system and unemployment. It was then that I realized what an incredibly intelligent and sharp mind Nick had. Of course, he didn't win the election — not even close. Having never worked with him on a campaign before, I was so disappointed! How could people not see what he had to offer our city? Nick, on the other hand, simply dusted himself off and moved on to the next demonstration or city hall meeting.

As far as Nick's other passion, sports, goes, I never really came to terms with the fact that he was never going to miss a CFL game in the summer — whether it was live or on television. I always felt a little put off when he would spend most weekend afternoons in front of the TV because, you see, I couldn't really do anything else in my apartment or our house while he was watching his games. He would be bellowing at the TV screen (or "coaching," as he called it), which made it much too noisy to read or concentrate on anything else!

I had always imagined myself having children. I knew that Nick had a daughter, Tegan, who lived with her mother in Montreal, and she would come and stay with him at Christmas and in the summer. I remember Nick taking me out one evening and telling me that he absolutely did not want to get married or have any more kids. I just nodded and in my naïve way decided that I could change his mind. Of course, anyone who knew Nick knows that once he's decided something he'll never change his mind! I have been blessed with grandchildren and have wonderful memories of time spent with them.

Nick's father died in 1990. He thought it made sense for us to live together rather than pay rent for two places, so we moved in together. He was still holding out on the marriage thing, insisting that it was an institution that he had no interest in being involved in. We were married three years later.

I can hardly remember a time when Nick didn't talk about wanting to write a book. He always talked about perhaps compiling the best of his letters to the editor (of which there are hundreds). When Nick was recovering in the hospital after his leg amputations, Victor Schwartzman, a retired human rights officer, writer and poet, began to visit him with exciting ideas for a book on Nick's life. Together they spent hours in the visitor's lounge or at Nick's bedside talking, with Victor taking notes and recording Nick's stories.

In 2010, a fourth year honours history student, Elliot Hanowski, who was taking an oral history course at the University of Winnipeg, chose Nick as his "subject" for his thesis. He taped a series of interviews with Nick about his life and transcribed them for him after he was done. Those transcripts were invaluable to the content of the book.

I am heartbroken that Nick couldn't be here to see the publication of his book. He was my best friend, and even though he had a hard time showing it, I knew that he loved me. But his body was so tired and I knew he couldn't wait any longer. He led an important life, unique and challenging, one that needed to be recorded. And so, here it is.

I want to thank the following people for being such an important part of Nick's life during the making of this book: Victor Schwartman, for giving Nick the spark he needed to take on this exciting project; Glenn Morison, for helping Nick apply for, and receive, a grant from the Manitoba Arts Council, for his patience in interviewing Nick (who could go on and on) and, of course, for helping Nick write the text of the book; Lawrie Cherniack, for his ongoing friendship and support for Nick throughout this process and for agreeing to write the Foreword; Donald Benham, whose ability to listen and give great "writer's" advice and ideas about the book often calmed Nick down; and Shirley Kowalchuck, a writer and a friend who believed that Nick had a book in him, before he even knew in what direction it would take him; and Judy and Tom Andrich, friends who were always there with smiles. Finally, I want to thank the people at Fernwood Publishing who made this book a reality: Wayne Antony, Nick's Managing Editor; Sandra McIntyre for structural editing; Jessica Antony for copy editing; Debbie Mathers for pre-production; Brenda Conroy for text design; Beverley Rach for production coordination; and John van der Woude for cover design.

1

Changes

"I may have become a lot shorter, with no legs, but it seemed the city saw me as a bigger man than I had ever been."

I was losing weight. I had gone off dairy and my doctor suggested this was the reason for the weight loss. I had no pain, no evidence of anything being wrong other than the weight loss and being slightly more tired than usual. I was eating well, starting each day with a brisk walk delivering papers. I was taking good care of myself. In June of 2005, I went to see a specialist in Celiac disease, a gluten-related disorder that can cause weight loss, among other symptoms. "It's quite possible that you have Celiac disease," the doctor said, "but we need a biopsy to be sure." The first step, he explained, would be a CAT scan. They took a CAT scan and the doctor phoned me back a week later. "Nick, we have a significantly bigger problem than Celiac," he said. "I think you have cancer."

We discussed hospitals and I said I didn't want to go to the Health Sciences Centre, the largest health care centre in Manitoba, mainly because I feared getting lost in the system. I wanted to go to a quieter place, so I chose the Grace Hospital. We went off to the Grace, and there they did a biopsy and a number of other tests and they determined that I had non-Hodgkin's lymphoma at the fourth stage. If I'd had any other kind of cancer I probably would have died already. Even in its last stages, this cancer is treatable.

"So long as we can treat it we will treat it." These were the words of Pat Harris, my oncologist. She is a tough woman. She told me she would not give up until there was no hope left, but if it got to that point, she would tell me. She was very blunt and she was very honest, but that meant she was also very clear. I knew I could trust her. The CancerCare nursing team also suggested I receive counselling from the social worker, whose office was just down the hall from them, as she was specially trained to help cancer patients and their families. The social worker was very helpful as there was just an overload of things in my mind and I didn't want to burden my wife, Emily, or any of my friends.

What followed were eight treatments of chemotherapy. I heard every horror story you could imagine about throwing up and wanting to stop treatments right away. Surprisingly, I tolerated chemo quite well and, after the first eight treatments, they told me I was in remission. Dr. Harris was clear though: this kind of cancer could easily come back. I learned to live with it. I realized that once you have cancer, you always have cancer and "remission" does not mean "cured." Within a few months of my diagnosis, I started calling myself a cancer survivor and decided to go public about it. My mother, who died of melanoma, thought her cancer was punishment from God. Melanoma was clearly deadly but, being very religious (Russian Orthodox), she did not undergo any treatment. She suffered for a very short period and then she died. Even though there were not as many treatment options in the 1980s as there are today, there were avenues she could have pursued. But she accepted the hierarchy and dogma of the Orthodox Church without question. She accepted the cancer as God's will. I didn't see it that way at all. She could have lived longer if she had not just accepted it.

Because of the shame of this perceived judgment, my mother was completely private about her illness. I was living in Calgary at the time and she didn't even tell me or my father of her illness until the very last stages. I could not accept that it was God's arbitrary judgment to inflict her with pain and suffering. She had grown up in Turkey and lived there until she was twenty-five. She loved the sun and played tennis and went to the beach a lot as a young person. There is very little doubt in my mind that her cancer was related to this exposure and nothing else.

When I read that close to fifty percent of all men and women are going to have some form of cancer in their lifetime, it seemed clear to me that going public was the right thing to do. It was more than just doing the opposite of what my mother did: I thought people could use the encouragement of how I was approaching it all and I was happy when the *Winnipeg Sun* did a series on my treatment. Laurie Mustard, a *Sun* columnist and former radio host, who was someone I had gone toe to toe with on a few issues in the past, made a habit of calling me and writing updates in the *Sun* so readers would know how I was doing. Mustard had been so impressed when I carried on with my paper route through my cancer, and I think he was more upset than I was when he came to visit me in the hospital. He was one of the first ones, at that time, to encourage me to get working on this book.

I also learned that cancer would likely overcome heart disease, within a few short years, as the most common life-threatening disease in Canada. In remission, I continued delivering newspapers for the *Winnipeg Sun*, writing my articles and being active politically. The cancer came back within a year. Even though I had to go to the hospital and get my blood tested constantly, it was still sudden when it returned. One week I didn't have cancer and the next week they said, "You've got cancer again." My doctor sent me to

Cancer doesn't stop Nick

the Health Sciences Centre for a seven-hour consultation. It felt like every doctor, nurse, therapist, social worker, pharmacist and counsellor in the building was getting a chance to weigh in on my case. I was very impressed with the collaborative approach. Far from being lost in the system, it was as if I had brought the entire system to my bedside.

They suggested a bone marrow transplant if I wanted to stop the cancer from coming back, and they gave me all the options. Number one, it was very important to get as close a match as possible. They told me my chances, ultimately, were sixty–forty if I went through with the bone marrow transplant: a sixty percent chance I would live; a forty percent chance I would die. I wanted better odds. I just wasn't prepared at that stage to go through that kind of thing, so I asked, "Well, what other treatments are there?" I could choose a different form of chemo treatment. My kind of cancer was very rare within the lymphatic non-Hodgkin's scope. They said only two percent of people get the same type of cancer. I really don't remember all the details of that day of poking and prodding. I can recall hearing "it is fast but slow." I had no idea what they meant by that. They told me that the best treatment was in Germany, where I was born, but they weren't prepared

Emily Ternette

to send me there. They were honest, telling me that even if it worked, the cancer could come back again. I heard about an RCMP officer that was going through his third treatment of chemo, beating this same form of cancer, but he was in very good physical shape. As I heard this, even though the first round had gone relatively well, it was hard to imagine taking three separate rounds of chemotherapy.

I talked to people who were comfortable talking to me. One was community activist and minister Harry Lehotsky. We had very different politics and had even had public debates at the Winnipeg Press Club on the legalization of prostitution where I was arguing in favour of legalization. In spite of our past differences, he was prepared to sit with me and hear me out. I returned the favour when he was diagnosed only a few years after me. I admired Lehotsky for his fundamental involvement in our city and I expect he admired me for similar reasons. I also liked that when his own diagnosis came, he said, "Why not me?" instead of "Why me?"

My wife, Emily, was my greatest support, hearing me out and helping me process all the information and choices that were rapidly coming my way. Emily was born with spina bifida and was never expected to walk. At the age of three she learned how to walk with the help of the children's rehab. She walked independently (even though her balance was never that great) until she broke her ankle in 1997. After that she began to use a walker and, eventually, because of damage done to her shoulders from falling, she began to use a power wheelchair.

I had met Emily in 1985, when she answered an ad for volunteer researchers for my TV show. I remember she sent me a full resume as if she were applying for a job. I knew a lot about her before we met and she was great at the researching job. (And so, it is true to say we met through

Nick and Emily on their wedding day

a newspaper ad.) I first met her face to face when I called together all the volunteers as a group at the restaurant Moskovitz & Moskovitz. I asked her out about two weeks later and we went to see a couple of German films at Cinema 3. She told me years later that she had a head cold that night and could not read the subtitles fast enough. She had no idea what the movies were about and was scared to death I would want to talk about the movies afterwards. Normally I would, but we didn't, and things worked out for us, perhaps because of that.

I met her parents a few months later and, because her dad was an architect and his firm was working on the Canadian Embassy in Moscow, her parents were very interested in my Russian background. So, that step took care of itself rather easily. We didn't move in together until 1990. I am very fortunate for all her support. Emily was working full time, making a reasonable living in 1995, and my part-time work added enough that we could afford to live, so that I had lots of time to do extra political work.

We come from different backgrounds. Emily's father, Ernest Smith, was a prominent architect in Winnipeg. He was the co-founder of Smith Carter in 1947 and Emily grew up knowing her father had created many of the landmarks around the city, including the Pan-Am Pool, the Richardson Building and the Centennial Centre. She also grew up with economic comfort that is foreign to my experience. She has supported my work and my political life ever since we have been together and the fact that she knew a different life than I did growing up has not been an issue for us. In fact, it rounds me out a little. I am sure it would have made the paper had

I ever been caught at one of the Smith family dinners at Rae and Jerry's Steakhouse!

Those dinners were a far cry from the dinner we had when I gave Emily her engagement ring. I had asked my friend Peter Warren if he could suggest a restaurant and he told me about a place up in an industrial area not far from Garden City. We wanted privacy so we got a booth but it was right next to the band and the drum was literally inches from our faces. Emily had to coach me on how to take out the ring and show it to her and formally propose and when I did, I was screaming over the top of the band. It was much less of an occasion than we hoped for.

Emily also likes to remind me that I left her standing several feet away at the wedding while I just smiled, admiring how great she looked. She had told me explicitly to meet her when her father walked her down the aisle because she was afraid she would be a little unsteady and nervous. I forgot. Other people like to tell stories about the wedding as well. I barely remember it, but am reminded of how I got tired of everyone who spoke about Emily's perseverance even with her disability and I stood up to tell everyone that what was more important to me was that "she had the most gorgeous body in the world." The bottom line is that I just wish we lived in a world that was more comfortable with, and more knowledgeable about, the various things we call disabilities. I greatly admire all the work that Emily has done in advocacy in this area but she is so much more than that. Even with these early obstacles and our fair share of challenges over the years, we have been together twenty-eight years and counting and she has helped me come a long way in acknowledging and allowing myself to feel instead of just think. Her patience has been a great gift to me and many, many people recognize what a special person she is. She has helped me to live with my many weaknesses and not be ashamed of or ignore my strengths.

It is a miracle when, even though I was born poor and I'm still poor, and my wife is poor, we managed to buy a house in Wolseley, at 158 Evanson, which is just across the lane from the house I lived in for six years on Lenore. Emily had inherited a small amount of money when her mother died and since we still didn't qualify for a mortgage at a bank we had to go to a finance company in order to get one. The house was in need of repairs. We paid $39,000 for it and once we fixed it up a bit, it was quite a step up from the apartment where we had been caretakers. We were bohemians and that was comfortable.

We decided that going for more treatments was my best option, and I started with four treatments in my second round of chemotherapy. The first two sessions were fine. I didn't even miss a day of work. I may have been dizzy, I may have had to go to bed right after six hours of treatment, but it was bearable. Then, starting with the third treatment, I was sick. After the tenth, I wanted to quit and the eleventh and twelfth were hell. I could not eat a thing. All the food smelled like cat urine. I just couldn't put anything in my mouth. I broke down. I couldn't sleep. Dr. Harris' message was clear: "You know, I don't think we're beating it," she said, and she suggested a new test, a major one, called the PET scan. She called it the gold standard of testing for cancer. It is a nuclear-radioactive CAT scan. Essentially, they put radiated sugar into your veins, and it goes through your body. When Dr. Harris saw the scan, I don't think she believed it herself, "You're free of cancer," she said. I was into remission again but then she decided to give me a drug that would try to stop the cancer from coming back. I went on Rituxan, which doesn't attack all your cells like other chemo, but it does lower your immune system drastically, so that infection and death were real possibilities. I may not have taken it, to be very honest, if I had fully understood that. I took it because it seemed the best way to keep the cancer away as long as possible. It worked remarkably, but in my case it blew out my immune system entirely. I got an infection in July of 2009. I had a little twinge in the bottom of my right foot, just a couple times at night-time. All I would have to do is twist my foot a little bit and the pain would go away. I knew that I hadn't broken a bone and there was no wound or anything to see so I tolerated it because I could walk perfectly fine. Every so often it would stab and hurt a bit. I never imagined it could be related to my cancer or the drug I was on, but I mentioned it to my family doctor and she couldn't see anything really wrong.

One night, close to the end of July 2009, my foot started to swell and the pain just took off. I knew that something was seriously wrong, so we went to the emergency department. In fact, we wound up going to four hospitals, because no one knew what to make of my symptoms, history and pain. Finally, at the Health Sciences Centre, they called in a specialist from the Infectious Diseases Clinic. The team treating me thought it was cancer and they were going to x-ray my foot again. The specialist came in, examined me, and said, "Don't you dare touch it!" It was necrotizing fasciitis, or so-called "flesh-eating disease." If they had moved me to do the x-ray they would have accelerated the disease, which didn't need any help in its vicious attack on my body. I might have died on the spot. The specialist also said anybody could catch flesh-eating disease and he could die himself if he touched it. "Don't you dare touch it!" His words still ring in my ears.

My choices were clear, amputation or death. I was pretty out of it by then and Emily was consulted over the phone by the specialist. In spite of being in shock, she said, "Of course, amputation." They nearly lost me. I don't think a closer brush with death is possible. I had the disease in both legs, so they had to amputate both. The flesh-eating disease eats the muscle from the inside. In my case, it was way inside the muscle, away from the nerves, which is probably why it caused so little pain. It can eat the heart muscle, it can eat the lungs, it can eat any tissue, though predominantly skin and muscle. Luckily, in my case, it started in the bottom of the leg and moved up. It didn't really stop but it slowed down on the way up, or I would not have survived. I had to have five more operations in order to make sure that it was clean and would not spread again and to ensure the healing of the wounds. It was at least six or seven weeks until they felt that the infection had gone. They never did find out where the infection began. They took all my teeth out, because I had some rotten teeth and they thought maybe the disease came from there. I was told by staff that during one of the operations something had gone wrong and I was given the wrong blood during a transfusion. Apparently, I was actually dead on the table for five minutes. I didn't remember any of this, of course, and when they told me about it, it was as if they were talking about someone else. In my first moments of consciousness after the first operation, I woke up in a dimly lit room. I could see only a few glowing red lights. My first thought was that I was in heaven, but before long I figured heaven would have to be better than a dimly lit room. So I next thought that I was in jail. Finally, I settled on the idea that I had been kidnapped. It was so real to me that I remember resolving to tell my kidnapper only one thing: my name. Maybe that is because I had no rank or serial number! As I continued to lie there in a fog, I saw what I called "a vision." An Aboriginal man with a beautiful feather headdress, in a wheelchair, with no legs, zoomed towards me. He came right up to me and then sped past me. After he disappeared, I felt peaceful. It was the strangest experience, but one I will never forget. Another thing I remember well: my good friend Peter Warren had called Emily out of concern. Hearing I had lost both my legs at the hip and all my teeth, he told Emily to tell me, "As long as Nick still has a mouth, he'll be fine!"

Even though I had various procedures, such as transfusions, all the time, they were risky. I lived knowing that I had already died once for five minutes and that what caused the trauma was still with me. I spent three and a half months in hospital. Two and a half months were just physically healing after the operations. You don't really want to stay in the hospital for too long because you can easily die of something that you catch there, like pneumonia. At least, that was my story. The care was great but hospitals are buildings full of disease. It is not where you want to be when you are trying to recover. My immune system was non-existent; normally I might have healed faster. They sent me off to the Rehabilitation Hospital to do the work and that was the good part. The rehab was excellent. Their job is to put you in a suitable wheelchair and then teach you how to dress, do exercises and maintain yourself. Within a month, they had worked me up to lifting a hundred pounds and I only weighed about a hundred and five.

In November 2009, I came out of rehab knowing I'd be in a wheelchair for the rest of my life. Emily and I had to make fundamental changes. We sold our house in Wolseley. We had to downsize. I lost the bottom half of my body and I had to get rid of about sixty percent of my belongings. And I was a pack rat. When I finally packed my files up, I found lunch receipts from 1976, a six-man football playbook from even before then and an embarrassing number of copies of the Coffee News that had an ad for my TV show in it. Fortunately, all my files and writing went to the archives at the University of Manitoba and were catalogued in the spring of 2012. When you get into your sixties and still have every school report card you ever received (including my five years of school in Germany), it just didn't seem right to toss them in the recycling bin.

The University of Winnipeg offered us a nice, accessible two-bedroom suite at McFeetors Hall, their student residence. There was a lot to like about living on campus, but it was a bit lonely for us. We both got out, but it could be work to do so. The physical facility was perfectly fine. Our neighbours were all busy students and we were a bit of an anomaly, two old geezers in wheelchairs. We could have been out on the street because there are not many suites accessible for two wheelchairs, in particular those with two accessible bedrooms (most have one). As most accessible suites are not made for more than one person in a wheelchair, Emily and I had to make sure changes were made to accommodate both of us. I knew of only one other family in Winnipeg that was also a family of two in wheelchairs. They don't build for two wheelchairs, and why would they? The University came through for us and we were very thankful. The media gave University President Lloyd Axworthy the credit. Lloyd and I had known each other since the late sixties, when he was one of my professors. We suspected he was responsible for securing us the suite. The alumni association was likely involved too.

I had not spent a night in hospital since I'd had my tonsils out as a nine-year-old, so the experience of being in hospital for three and half months led me to write more, and I received all sorts of unexpected feedback from the writing. Even through both my courses of cancer treatment, I was always an outpatient. I wrote six feature columns for the *Winnipeg Sun*. I got tremendous feedback from the hospital community. There were complaints, as some did not like what I wrote. Nurses told me stories about administrative policy and I wrote about that but I spoke well of the staff, who had to work under the conditions that really needed to be exposed.

People approached me to say thank you very much for the articles about hospitals. I shared an experience that most people never have and never want to have, but that doesn't mean they weren't curious. I was overwhelmed by the mail I received. We had set up a trust fund to cover all the extra costs we faced and, unbelievably, the cards poured in and the money poured in. By the time we closed the trust fund in February, we had raised close to thirty thousand dollars. I certainly never had that kind of response when I was running for mayor! Who would have imagined that we could raise that much? There were a few anonymous donors who gave one thousand dollars or so, but most people gave twenty-five or thirty or fifty dollars and it added up. I didn't know what to say and most people said that "Nick Ternette" and "speechless" didn't belong in the same sentence! Emily and I thanked everybody publicly in letters to the *Winnipeg Free Press,* and *Free Press* columnist Gordon Sinclair did a piece on our gratitude.

One letter that stuck with me was from Francisco Valenzuela-Guevara:

> Sorry for sending you this very modest contribution [for the record, it was not that modest, actually] but we are in a half-pension plan only. The main thing is to wish you a healthy recovery and continue

your commitment to the society. Let me write a few lines in my own English in order to explain why, why we care about you. For long years, we shared similar activities in Winnipeg. But I have never tried to start a personal contact with you during our marches along the streets or political-cultural meetings. I do read your interesting letters to the editor. I also send letters once in awhile. I came here as a refugee after I spent two years in the filthy military jails of dictator Pinochet in Chile. I was chief of police in Santiago for democratic president Allende, and commander in army forces as well but I was washing dishes and cleaning floors here a few years ago. However, I was active as a volunteer for the Manitoba Federation of Labour, the Labour Choir, Manitoba Solidarity with Cuba, helping an election campaign for Howard Pawley, and the Chilean Association. I wish we had more resources to cooperate more to you now that you need it. We, we admire what you do and it disgusting that they never considered your name for the Order of Manitoba, something you deserve. Recover and continue writing your comments in the Free Press.

Leslie and Eric Bray expressed a sentiment that was surprisingly, even amazingly, common:

When I caught my initial glimpse of the headline in Gordon Sinclair's article, my heart felt so happy for you. My hubby and I are thrilled about the support you are getting as well as the honours and credits for all you do for the people of Winnipeg and Manitoba. You often give us new ideas to consider and some understanding of what "really is going on." Today's picture of Emily and you, Nick, is inspiring, along with the article: Bravo to a couple who is a great example of someone surmounting huge obstacles in life. Wishing you all the best in your life in a new home, I think you'll be a great asset for the students, and they for you.

I must have received more than two hundred letters that fall. Most of them were simple, to the point and very kind, just like the Brays' letter. The thirty thousand dollars in the trust fund paid for a lot of equipment and some new furnishings that fit into our new home. We had to revitalize some furniture and replace other stuff as we downsized. Just about every day someone stopped me when I was drinking a tea or on the bus and said, "Hey, you're Nick Ternette." These were people I'd never met let alone spoken with. "You are the one who, you know, has written the articles about civic politics," they would say. "I don't always agree with you, but I respect you and admire you for the work that you have done." That was the general tone of a lot of people. It was overwhelming. I know many people thought I was crazy. I'd been verbally attacked and labelled more times than I could count. I had spent my life, for the most part, feeling completely neglected. Throughout my forty years in Canada, I'd been called a communist, a shit-disturber who should be put in jail, a Nazi and a fascist. All of a sudden, out of the blue, I was "an institution," as Emily called it. I may have become a lot shorter, with no legs, but it seemed the city saw me as a bigger man than I had ever been. Susan Thompson, who I had opposed constantly when she was mayor, called me "an historic figure" and a person, "that should have a park named after him." I took it seriously in the sense that they were sincere but, truth be told, I had not accomplished that much in Winnipeg. I tried, and I'll grant you that I stuck it out when others walked away, but I know an awful lot of people who have accomplished a lot more and they remain completely unknown to the public. Some of the same people shaking my hand and smiling the day I received my distinguished alumni award at the University of Winnipeg had it in their job description to watch over my organizing work on campus in the seventies, to make sure it never got out of hand. I also had to remember this was the same school that banned me from campaigning on campus during one of my runs at mayor.

Some of the new reactions were just silly. People seemed amazed that I took the bus. They said, "How can you take the bus, don't you go on the…" and then they didn't know what to say. They realized they were telling me I was disabled. In many ways, it showed people's widespread and profound ignorance about disability. "How do you get around? You take a taxi constantly?" They all knew about Handi-Transit and asked about that too. I said, "No, I take the bus, as I always did when I had my legs!" And they just didn't believe me. Some even argued. The conversations could be crazy. Strangers asked me, "What are you doing out in the rain?" They couldn't believe that I was out constantly. Sure, I fell out of the wheelchair one winter and flipped over. My wheelchair went in one direction and I hit my head on the other side — luckily there was snow and I didn't hurt myself. I just waited for someone to help me back into my chair. For this people talked to me as if I were a hero.

As soon as I was well enough, I exercised. I realized immediately that I had to maintain my upper body strength, especially for transferring in and out of my wheelchair. Professor Jim Silver, a very good friend of mine at the University of Winnipeg, helped me get a free membership card at the University's fitness centre, where I went once I was done with rehab. It took a while for me, but finally I got a personal trainer who was so pleased that somebody like me wanted to keep my body in shape. There I was with no legs, working out as hard as I ever had, and enjoying it! I suffered from depressive episodes. Exercise helped stave off the episodes. But of course when I was down, exercise was all the harder to do.

I stayed busy with other things besides just keeping healthy and staying alive. When Emily could no longer work and went on her pension, I started to volunteer at Winnipeg Harvest, in part because I could take some food home at the end of my shift. It was hard work, hauling the heavy food around. I started with the food packing. Later, I joined their Education Committee, which was where I stayed because I could no longer pack food. I was on the Editorial Committee of their newspaper, *The Better Times*, which informs those most affected by poverty about some of the ongoing issues. It took a while to get the paper running but we tried to get a print run of six thousand copies out five or six times a year.

Then, in 2010, I was elected to the Provincial Council of the Manitoba League of Persons with Disabilities. I was chair of the Transportation Committee, dealing with Handi-Transit and buses and related matters. I was more interested in disability issues, obviously, than I had been in the past, but because of my health issues I had trouble meeting the demands of the position. I was still the master of ceremonies at May Day each year. I continued to go to every demonstration there was.

I wasn't writing regularly for anybody but sometimes I would get riled up and just have to write a letter or an article. I put out "The Ternette Report" (also the name of my TV show at one point), which was sent by email to 750 interested people to let them know what had been published and where, as well as upcoming left-wing events. Prior to that, in 2007 and 2008, I put out a little newsletter called *Left Punch* and was blogging at *Bravejournal*, where my posts were more personal than political. Before that I had a newsletter called "The Left Fax."

In 2010, I was given the Distinguished Alumni Award from the University of Winnipeg, during their June convocation. This is essentially an honorary degree. I had to sit with the establishment. It was a little surreal. The standing ovation that I got was truly overwhelming. In the context of all the abuse and insults thrown my way over the years, it was dreamlike. They told me it lasted two minutes. Emily cried. I had time to look around; I saw mothers, fathers, grandmothers and grandfathers of those who were graduating, and I had known them from coaching sports, some political event or maybe even the music scene. This wasn't scoring a goal or a touchdown, they were applauding my life. It was a very odd experience and I still don't know quite what to make of it.

The secretary who I worked with at the Neighbourhood Services Centre forty years ago ran up to me and gave me a great big hug. So many people from my past came up and said something. It was like that TV show from the fifties, *This Is Your Life*.

The most remarkable thing of all is a letter handed to me by former mayor Susan Thompson, who was in charge of the University of Winnipeg Foundation at the time:

Dear Mr. Ternette,

I'm very pleased to read of the Distinguished Alumni Award bestowed on you by the University of Winnipeg. It has encouraged me to make a donation to the University for the Carl Ridd Scholarship in the Humanities Fund. For personal reasons, this donation is to remain anonymous as to the source. Let me explain. I'm a Holocaust survivor, and still suffer the effects of my youth spent years in various concentration camps. Forget I cannot. Forgive only on an individual basis. You were born just as the war was close to coming to an end. It was the period when the transports to the gas chambers were accelerated so as to make the world as *Judenrein* ["free of Jews"] as possible. Of course, none of this was of your doing. More importantly and in contrast, you have demonstrated throughout your life a level of humanness that is the farthest opposite of that prevailing in your country of birth when you came into this world. You have always fought for the poor and disadvantaged. You have supported programs and policies designed to improve the well-being of our community, regardless of race, religion or ethnicity.

You are what we call in Yiddish a *mentch* [a very good person]. And you know from which language that word was borrowed, with a different spelling. Judaism recognizes the importance of meaningful names. Its mystical tradition works with the letter values of names. When I write your name and that of your beloved Emily and assign you corresponding values to each consonant, it resolves in the number two hundred and thirty-four; thus the initial amount of my gift. As Jews wish each other until one-twenty, that being the age at which our great teacher Moses passed away, I add two times one-twenty, two-forty is the amount for a total four hundred and seventy-four dollars. [So, he contributed four hundred and seventy-four dollars to the Carl Ridd Scholarship in the Humanities Fund.] Thank you for all the good work done to date. Despite the setbacks you have endured and continued to feel, may both of you have many more years together in happiness.

Your anonymous, grateful friend and admirer

The only way I could respond was with a letter to *The Jewish Post*. I felt overwhelmed with emotions when I read that letter. I have never received anything like this in forty years of activism, especially in view of the fact that I am a German-Canadian and the donor was Jewish and a Holocaust survivor.

In May of 2012, I was invited to a conference in Toronto about the Guaranteed Annual Income. I was very happy to go and really appreciated the opportunity. When I arrived, however, I found that my wheelchair had been smashed beyond use and I had to wait at the airport while a replacement was found. While I was in Toronto, they fixed mine so I could go home with it, but all the anxiety and discomfort over a simple thing like going to a meeting was something I had not imagined happening to me when I was only sixty-seven.

Honestly, it is very difficult being so constrained. The issues with my immune system are more limiting than not having any legs. I need to be on constant watch for infection so I have to take my temperature every night. A slight fever could mean that I am dying. I have to say no to so many things I would like to do because I am tired or run down or sick people might be there; I can't go or I am taking a huge risk. I have had depressions throughout my life relating to various situations, but the last few years have been worse than any other time. I have seen counsellors and I try to be thankful for what

I am able to do but I'd be fooling myself if I tried to tell others that this has been a seamless transition for me. I had imagined, as I worked so hard at my rehab, that life would be back to normal once I was done. It isn't that way.

There are still people saying, "Why aren't you running for mayor in this election?" and I say, "I've retired! For more than six years. Come on!" But, they keep saying, "You're the one who raises issues, you're the one who is out in the front, and you've got to keep on doing it." Somehow, I have to hold this in my mind along with all the recognition and praise from the establishment that has come since I lost my legs. When I retired, the mayor gave me a big letter of thanks for the citizens' advocacy that I carried out over the years. Some of my friends are laughing and saying, "Oh, Nick, you're just being bought off, you know!" I said, "No, I'm not being bought off. They are sincere in their thoughts. They like my retirement because I won't be on their case anymore." Retirement is a funny thing and it brings out odd comments and actions. My father got a little watch when he retired from the hospital after nineteen years. I didn't get a watch but I have had all these honours and accolades from my opponents.

I am a socialist, a Marxist and an anti-capitalist. I haven't given up my views, and won't ever. Whatever I can do, I do! I don't go to all the planning meetings or organizing meetings anymore; simply put, I have to rest at times. I can only do about two or three hours of work at one time, so my writing has declined too.

I retired from running for office in 2002. Running for office twenty times, both here and in Calgary, should be enough for anyone. Retiring from civic politics didn't mean retiring from life. Now there are no timelines. Everything I do, I do by choice. A good retirement works that way and it is still working for me.

I don't think anybody really retires anymore. Many people can't afford to retire because their pensions are simply too small. They never earned much of a CPP, and their old age income and whatever else they might have just isn't enough. They have to work. There are people that are seventy or seventy-five who still work for pay! The word "retirement" is going to have to change. I grew up watching people retire at sixty-five and die at seventy. I have been told, and I agree, that we die the way we live. I wasn't going to quit marching. I wasn't going to quit being me. There are too many people that, while they claim they're socialists or radicals or whatever else, if you look at their performance you see they never show up. They don't live their ideas out. I'm not putting them down, it's just not what I have done. I've tried to be what I say I am, a radical. In my twenties, I called myself a revolutionary because, as young people, we dream about revolution. I dreamed about revolution all the time, but the reality is something different. We thought a revolution was going to happen. This is probably not unlike some Christians who believe that Christ is coming back any day. In the last twenty years, I have never once called myself a revolutionary. I am a radical and an activist. I heard some young people using the word "slacktivist" for a person who "speaks out" with the clicking of the mouse by signing on-line petitions. I never want to be one of those. Activists are active. It's not complicated.

An activist is concerned about issues that affect the community, like the violence in the West End where I now live. We need to gain control of our streets. It matters and it is right here in front of our eyes. These "in your face" issues are important. I intend to stay active in these ways until I die. I may not be the marshal or have the bullhorn in my hand but I will support the twenty-year-olds, ten-year-olds and all those who are struggling for liberation of their own kind. We live in a capitalist society and we understand that revolution is not going to happen until a massive amount of people get involved and risk a brand new world. I don't see it happening in my life but it will come eventually. I still accept the Marxist logic of "the dialectic," which means societies go from feudalism to primitive capitalism to industrial capitalism to post-modern capitalism. Although Marx didn't talk about that, he did recognize that there will be changes in capitalism, and no matter what permutations of it we face, ultimately it will lead to some form of socialism and ultimately the utopia of the *Communist Manifesto*! Socialism will rise some day. It may be a hundred years from now and if that is when then that is fine. I don't need to see it, and many other contemporary socialists will never see it. When I was young, I believed in revolution. Now, I believe in evolution. Socialism is the only way we're going to survive. Otherwise, climate change will destroy us. Either we move towards cooperative, smaller and healthier communities to live in, or we're going to die. People like James Laxer, the founder of the Waffle movement, who ran for the leadership of the NDP, are talking about cities having to shrink to one third their size because there will be no oil left, and all transportation will have to be public. In the long run, whether it's twenty-five, fifty, or a hundred years from now, there will be some form of socialism evolving in our country, and in all likelihood, around the world.

The environment is always going to be at the core of politics. Given my situation, environmental health is my passion now. I expect to die from an environmental cancer related to the use of pesticides.

David Nickarz, who is known for fighting the whaling industry and who developed testicular cancer, which also is an environmental cancer, asked me to form the Cancer Brigade to raise awareness about the environment and cancers. Surgery and chemotherapy cured his cancer but left him dealing with numerous side effects for the rest of his life. We worked with a school-teacher named Dianne Harms. We did this for about two years. The media paid some attention to the linkage between using pesticides and cancer. In fact, the trend is away from environmental-based research as the companies that produce the toxins are often the very ones that run the various ribbon campaigns to raise money for cancer research. This was very well documented in a recent movie called *Pink Ribbon, Inc.* This is another reason this work is so important. It is complicated and, as usual, the whole story never gets out. CancerCare Manitoba has said that non-Hodgkin's lymphatic cancer has a higher than average per-capita occurrence in Manitoba and in New Brunswick, the two Canadian provinces that use the most pesticides. In the Maritimes, it is for potato crops and, sadly, in Manitoba, the most common use is for weeds like dandelions. Before I die, I expect CancerCare to go on record linking pesticides directly to at least this form of cancer.

Every other city in North America, except New York, has banned malathion for use in spraying against mosquitoes. It is a carcinogen. It is not that they don't still spray for mosquitoes, but they do not use malathion, because they all recognize that it causes cancer. We are up against the mythology that has been built. "Ah, kill those mosquitoes!" you know? People don't give a damn what it does to you. Opinion polls say that ninety percent of people want to be sprayed and want to kill mosquitoes, even if it causes five or six cancers and sixty thousand dollars in treatment for each one of us. It is easy to say that when you are not the one sitting in a wheelchair with no legs and waiting for your primary cancer to resurface and kill you.

2

The Making of an Activist

"I saw police taking students … and beating them with clubs. My reaction was to meet militancy with militancy."

I was born in January 1945, in Berlin, to Seraphine Huntzinger, named after an angel in the Russian tradition, and Georg Ternette. It was the end of the Second World War and the Allies were smashing and destroying Berlin on a daily basis. It would be an understatement to say I was born on the wrong side of the world's tracks.

As my mother describes it, "you were born in a hospital and we survived." My mother told me that in those early days, when the bombs were falling all over the place, she would take me to the basement of our apartment. All of us went down there. The block was nine stories high and had four sections surrounding a central courtyard. The bombing was part of everyday life. I was also told about the time a bomb actually penetrated the basement of the apartment block where we lived but my mother had not made it downstairs. At least six or seven people died, because they used bombs that splintered and the splinters would fly in every direction. I also know that my mother's best friend was blown up by a bomb when they were out walking, and that she was so isolated she had to sometimes leave me all alone in our apartment when she had to go to the store or run an errand. Although I don't remember these early years myself, I have lived my entire life knowing this is how my life started.

I was an only child and my parents were not the least bit demonstrative with each other. Somehow, at age twenty-six, my mother had made her way from Turkey to Berlin, where she met my father. Her father had provided for her, but he had died, and this must have been what prompted the move. It must have been quite an odyssey during wartime. My father was an ethnic Russian serving in the German army and was away much of the time. My mother became pregnant during a furlough. I was four years old before I ever met my father. He had been captured by the Russians and kept in a

Georg and Seraphine Ternette, Nick's parents

prison camp. The Russians used him as forced labour doing translation after the war until he was released in 1949.

My mother never talked about my father and I believe she thought he was dead and was looking forward to collecting a widow's pension. Suddenly, he arrived on the home doorstep. In truth, the marriage had been one of economic necessity for my mother. It was the pressure of the church that kept them from divorcing, for I never remember seeing any intimacy or even kindness between the two of them. I do know there were different men around the house in those years before my father returned. I don't think my mother had the life she dreamed of.

My earliest personal memories come from age three or four. I remember wandering around our neighbourhood and I could see the ruins all over the place. There was our apartment block and then there was nothing — for a stretch of blocks, nothing but ruins. I can also picture people starting to clean up. Either way it is a fantastic sight in my memory. How could they have taken four years to start cleaning up? How were these old women in babushkas ever going to clean up this mess one stone at a time?

In 1948, when I was three, the Soviets erected the Berlin Blockade. I remember going to our church, the Russian Orthodox Church, to get medical supplies and clothing. The Russians had blockaded Berlin completely and the Americans were flying in all these supplies and dropping them in Berlin. I do not remember ever seeing the planes, but I remember my mother dragging me to the church basement where we would get clothing and other supplies that the Americans threw out of the planes.

I wasn't really a Berliner. I spoke Russian before I spoke any other language. My parents were both Russian, originally from St. Petersburg, known at the time as Stalingrad. Other kids in Berlin didn't really understand who I was. They knew that I was Russian and the Russians were the bad guys.

Nick as a child in Berlin

Even in that kind of environment, Berlin was a fascinating city. My father had a small potato farm in what became East Berlin. When the fences went up in 1948, we no longer had access to it. I also had a cousin in East Berlin. I have pictures of her holding me as a child, but once the fence and then the wall went up, we couldn't see her. We had no other family around either.

Another memory from a very young age is going to the potato farm with my dad where there were Russian soldiers all over the place speaking Russian. What did I know about politics? I was a young child, I heard and understood people speaking my language and I wanted to talk with them. I remember my dad panicking and telling me *never* to talk to the soldiers. Befriending the occupiers was not a wise thing to do?

Most of my life outside of school was spent at the church where we were around other Russians. The faith was the centre of my mother's life. I was an altar boy and helped the priests. I loved being an altar boy. It was theatre to me — the dressing up — and knowing what to do on cue was a source of pride and happiness. Even when services would last three or four hours, I was happy to be part of them even when I was just six or seven. In one long service, when I was likely no older than five, I peed myself, soiling the robe I was wearing and embarrassing my mother greatly. What I remember is that I really wanted to be a priest. Even at home, I would dress up in robes and pretend I was a priest. The church had a rule that no woman could go near the communion table. I remember one time — I couldn't have been any older than ten — yelling at a woman and lecturing her for standing too close to the altar. What I remember more was the priest yelling at me; if I recall correctly, the gist of it was that the woman was wrong but it was his job to yell at the women, not mine.

I cringe when I think what I might have become if I had stayed in the church. Becoming a priest would most likely have meant being ruthless and dominating. I left the church in my teens and that is something my mother never forgave me for. I imagine she died thinking that her husband and son were both going to hell, perhaps along with herself. The Orthodox Church always struck me as having its whole life rooted in fear. The church was a place where I could speak and hear my mother tongue, Russian, and that was its only appeal for me as I got older and realized how controlling the church was. My dreams of the priesthood died at a young age.

When I entered school, I wasn't very much liked. Some of the kids knew I was Russian and the Russians had won the war. Who knows what parents said in their houses? We now know of the atrocities that went along with the Russian victory. Germans were hostile towards Russians, understandably so. I was a loner by circumstance, not choice. When I was nine years old, about a year before I left Berlin, the kids on the street were building forts with the rubble that was still there. We used stones to play cowboys and Indians, and we would have a fort to defend ourselves. I was always an Indian because I was never allowed to win. One time, they did not just play cowboys and Indians; they actually stuffed me in the fort and closed the opening with more stones. I couldn't open it from the inside. They buried me alive. I was in there for at least an hour and a half. As I recall, my mother finally started searching for me. The police dug me out; my mother must have called them. I probably was not in real danger of dying, but it is a story that sums up my childhood in Berlin. I knew marginalization from very early on in my life.

On Sunday afternoons, and only on Sunday afternoons, we went to the movie house. They were all American movies — westerns and comedies mostly — with German voiceovers. I remember realizing that later. My favourites were Laurel and Hardy. There was also a small puppet theatre where my parents took me. Enjoying them is about as fond a memory as I can conjure from those first ten years of my life. In fact, one of my fondest memories of childhood is when my mother bought me my own marionettes to play with. I was about eight or nine. My hobby, which I spent hours and hours on, was collecting and trading comic books.

Having only met my father after his prison camp years, I have no idea what he might have been like before that time. He was a meek and quiet man around my mother. Between this strange home life and a lack of friends of any kind, I can't say there is much happiness to recall from the first ten years of my life. Not many people would describe me as warm or intimate and, no doubt, this relates to the type of home where I grew up.

I had not really sorted out what it meant to be a Russian living in post-war Germany; then, at the age of ten, I went from being hated by Germans to being seen as a German in post-war Canada. My life as the outsider took a big twist. While I can't remember every thought, I know I wanted to be less different than I was, but that seemed impossible. While I know this figures into who I came to be, it has never been clear to me exactly how. I have done anything but be "less different" or "fit in" in any sense of those words. More likely what this constant marginalization, combined with somewhat distant parents, produced was a sense that I would have to develop my own security in the form of a very thick skin. I truly am not bothered by criticism and don't personalize all the insults and rejections that have been hurled my way. I could not have lived the life I have without imperviousness to criticism.

If I am misunderstood, it is precisely on this issue. I can get caught up in a cause and some people think, "It's all about Nick" and that I just want to see my name in print. Friends have even used the phrase, "turn off the Nick switch." I am truly interested in neither criticism nor praise. If you buy into one, you buy into the other. It has been a little amusing being spoken of so nicely in my older years, but it is the ideological commitment to speak into a debate biased to the right that kept me going.

My father had been in Canada for a year when my mother and I finally joined him. We flew from Berlin to Hamburg and from there took a steam ship to Montreal where we boarded the train to Winnipeg. I can picture the playroom they had for kids on the boat and remember that the train ride across Canada seemed very long.

I had whooping cough when I was young and spent months away from school. I had bronchitis and perhaps asthma too. Berlin's climate is like

Vancouver or Victoria. When I came to the dryness of Winnipeg, there was great improvement. I had not imagined this benefit before coming.

I only spoke a few words of English when we arrived in Winnipeg so I couldn't start at Laura Secord School right away. I went to a special class on Colony Street, in the building that is now the adult education centre. There were about twenty-five of us and I was the only German. I remember there being mostly Italians, and a few Serbs. I did well and entered Grade 6 at Laura Secord the next year, meaning I did not lose any time because I had only completed Grade 4 in Germany. I ended up going to high school at Daniel McIntyre instead of Gordon Bell because I could take German instead of Latin there. School was hard enough so I took a slightly easier route.

I spent my first three or four summers at Grand Beach where my mother would rent a cabin and my father would come on his days off. My first summer, I collected bottles all summer and, at the end, turned them in and made $12. I call that my first job and I remember depositing all of it when I opened my first bank account. I spent my days at Grand Beach with my mother or riding bikes with my father all the way to Bird's Hill Park. My preteen years were more about keeping busy than really enjoying myself. I had one good friend, Bob Smith, who introduced me to the North American sports that were all new to me. We spent a lot of time together but he moved to Vancouver after Grade 9.

Baptists had supported my parents financially in getting to Canada and I know that the first place we lived was the top storey of a three-bedroom house at 127 Canora Street. My father wanted to go to the Baptist Church because of their help, but my mother remained strong in the Orthodox tradition and called him a "traitor" for even thinking of a switch. My father also worked hard to repay the Baptist Church for their support. He worked on an extra gang for the railway making eighty cents a day working ten-hour days, six days a week.

To be honest, when I first came to Canada at the age of ten, I knew nothing about German history, especially about the Nazi period, because my parents didn't tell me anything. Then I experienced anti-German racism, when children began to bully me by calling me a squarehead and a Nazi. I had to learn my history and background quickly. I also started to develop my thick skin at that age. When my father saw the kids chasing me around and calling me those names and me getting angry and chasing them back, he said, "that is exactly what they want, ignore them and they will stop." He was right. I ignored them and they stopped and so it was that at that young age I learned not to let the foolishness of others get to me and, given the life I led, it was a good lesson to learn.

Throughout my life, I've had to deal with the issue of German guilt. This is the thought that by virtue of being German, you are responsible for the Holocaust. There is no simple answer. I wasn't a Nazi. I have had close German friends who did fight and many of those young kids who fought, died. I think many of the surviving Nazis had as much guilt about surviving as they did about being Nazi. My father was in a concentration camp in Russia for four years. Even though my mother never spoke about the war, in my teenaged years, my father began talking about it, and could talk about it forever. It is like Holocaust survivors: some never talk about it and others never stop. My father was proud because he had won the First Class Iron Cross and he did great things to survive in the camp. The stories lost their impact when you heard them repeatedly. It wasn't something he could really find people wanting to hear about here in Canada so my mother and I were his audience. He was never a Nazi. He was an interpreter from Russian to German for the German intelligence and then he worked in a prison camp after the war interpreting for the Russians and was kept one year after the armistice in 1948 because of his unique language skills.

Aside from the church, I don't recall my parents having a social life in Winnipeg. When I was older, the priests would call for tea or even a meal, and there were events in the Russian community, but visitors to our home were rare. My mother was pretty much a loner. A reasonably talented painter, she needed to be completely alone when she wanted to paint. Sometimes I would have to go out so she could have the apartment to herself.

I loved sports but I was never very good. I just didn't have a particularly athletic build. With the encouragement of several good teachers at Daniel McIntyre High School, I wound up working as a sports broadcaster in high school. I worked with Vince Leah, Fred Collins and Jack Wells broadcasting high school football games on CJOB Radio. I was the chief statistician. I would feed them information as they needed it. I sat in the press box up in the football stadium. It was quite a break for a teenage immigrant. They even paid me a little bit. Kas Vidruk, who had played for the Bombers for many years and had been known for beginning his pro career at age seventeen, sent me a letter thanking me for all this work I was doing for high school football. He included a fifteen-dollar cheque as an honorarium. I wound up doing the same for basketball; I covered all the basketball games and sent reports to the papers and radio stations. When I told Jack Wells that I wanted to be a sports reporter on the radio he said, "Yeah, well, you should go to the national radio school on Portage Avenue and be trained." When I went there, they said to me, "You've got to get rid of your accent. You can't do anything; you will never be allowed to do any broadcasting until you get rid of your accent." I know what I said back. I said, "I'm not getting rid of my accent, that's me, who I am," I walked out — that was it! Career over before it started. I was in a tough place because I did not want to be different yet I knew who I was, and I had to be true to that as well. The carryover from those days is a life-long interest in sports and a friendship with Vince Leah that lasted until he died in 1993.

I had a major drop in my marks in Grade 11. I went from being a B+ student to failing. I got a 60 in German — that has to tell you something was not right! I just found other things more interesting than schoolwork. I was involved in the debating club, called the Phoenix Society, sports, the model parliament, the yearbook and the school newspaper. I particularly liked the Model United Nations. Because I could speak Russian, I represented Russia and I remember picking up books from the Co-op Book Shop to prepare to offer the Russian perspective. We debated things like the U.S. gunboats in the Caribbean, the apartheid policies of South Rhodesia and U.N. membership for the People's Republic of China. If there was a single moment where the political world opened up to me, the Model U.N. was it.

My mother got very upset about my drop in marks and she decided to send me off to the military one summer. It was my mother who raised me, as she dominated my father and he worked all the time, in part, I guess, to be away from her. He would bring his money home and turn it over to her and she would give him an allowance to live on. My home was quiet. Occasionally Russians would come over and make a little noise drinking vodka but my parents were both teetotallers so that was not common.

I was also a counsellor at Camp Manitou and Camp Stevens, jobs I got from the experience of my training with the YMCA. I worked with the YMCA as they had been very good at providing leadership, but my mother had decided to send me off to the Young Soldiers Training Plan, a short-lived plan in the late 1950s and early 1960s meant to draw people into the service. I had to go to the Minto Barracks for initial training and then I went by train to Brandon, then on to Camp Shilo, where the camp was held.

At army camp, I learned first aid. I learned how to make beds. I also learned, however, to shoot guns, which I hated. I used to carry Sten guns and Bren guns. These are submachine guns, which they made out of five dollars' worth of steel. I was a terrible shot. I hated everything about the camp. I hated obeying orders. I refused to salute people. I was on the outs much of the time. Because I knew sports, I was the ump for baseball and refereed other sports. That was about the only thing that worked out for me.

The army officers punished me a lot. They forbade me to go home. I had to clean the barracks. I had to shine my shoes and then shine them again. I marched better than I shot and I probably was told that every day. If I had finished, I could have entered the regular army. It would not have worked out. They used to get mad at me because I would carry the gun the wrong way, saying, "You'll kill somebody with it like that!" Even though I had no bullets, you had to follow instructions or they yelled at you. I just didn't think like they did. My only way to get back at some of them was allowing the close calls to those that I didn't like when I umpired or refereed some of the sports. I found it funny much of the time but I was happy to leave when my mother changed her mind and brought me back to go to summer school and to pick up some of the classes I had failed.

That summer taught me to dislike the army and to dislike authority. I just didn't like the saluting and everything that went with it. I was a contrary guy. I liked being a rebel for amusement's sake. It was not political then, it was personal. My high school yearbook said "Nick likes to argue" and I still do! The only difference is that now I know why I am arguing.

My mother's attitude was pretty much, "Get a steady job. You know, you're not a student, you really don't like studying." It would be an understatement to say that she wasn't a very encouraging person. She would stand up for me, like the time she went to local journalist Shaun Herron's house and lambasted him for things he wrote about me in his *Winnipeg Free Press* column. Many times she threw Russian friends out of the house when they asked her how she ever could have raised her only kid to be a communist. But while she supported me outside the house, as I grew up and even as an adult, she was always critical.

For me, however, it was clear that I was going to go to university. Even at that age, I had learned to dust off my mother's criticism. I had two teachers who were supportive. One was Ken Osborne, who worked with me in the Phoenix Club where we learned about debating. He went on to a robust career in the Faculty of Education at the University of Manitoba until his retirement in 1996. He still writes on education for the *Winnipeg Free Press* and elsewhere. He was active in the NDP and I have enjoyed bumping into him over the years, always thankful for the encouragement he gave to me in my teens. The other was Johnny Potter, who was a sports coach, counsellor and vice principal. He also encouraged me to pursue university. I kept up with him too until he passed away in the fall of 1999. He coached high school football in Winnipeg for over forty years and was inducted into the Manitoba Sports Hall of Fame.

I wanted to go to United College, which is now the University of Winnipeg. My marks were not good but they were good enough to get in and I had some savings of my own from the military experience. As I went through university, I had one summer shining shoes at the Elmhurst Golf and Country Club followed by two summers with Co-op Implements, assembling farm machinery in Transcona.

My first year of university was rough. There was no real discipline; you didn't have to attend classes if you didn't want to attend classes. It created chaos in my life.

Interestingly, I always liked structure (though not structure imposed for authoritarian rule, like the army). Perhaps it was a "German" trait? My wife says I have "obsessive compulsive disorder" and she has lived with me for twenty-four years! Others have suggested to me that I might have Asperger's Syndrome, meaning that I am a highly functioning autistic. It makes a little sense because I have never been too worried about my physical appearance, have issues with intimacy and need predictability, order and structure more than most people do. Back then, they didn't diagnose things like that so it wasn't really an issue. Now, at my age, what good would a diagnosis of some kind do? We all cope with who we are, that's life. The unpredictable life at university made for a hard time at first, but I did well enough to pass and then, later on, I hit my stride. There were a couple of especially good professors in the Sociology Department at the University of Winnipeg. Myron Utech and Katherine George, who was a Marxist and a member of the

Communist Party, are two that I can single out for grabbing my imagination. Professor George was a very bright woman who had fled the States during the McCarthy era. In her class, I liked the Russian-American sociologist Pitirim Sorokin, whom she loathed, so I chose to write essays praising him. I was always a contrarian and she gave me bad marks because I chose to be that way. A few years later, I wrote to her when I was in Europe with the radical student movements, and out of that we developed a friendship. It was only afterwards that I came to hear that she suffered from mental illness and eventually took her own life. The University of Winnipeg has a sociology scholarship in her name. I also met Werner Goetze in my second year. He was fifteen years older than me, but he was German and we first connected that way. He remained one of my best friends until he died in March of 2000.

Another friend from those days who I still keep in touch with is Bart Sacrule. Bart was raised in Trinidad and came to Winnipeg via England. Between his colour and my accent, we both stuck out in our own ways. We met through the young Liberals and spent quite a bit of time together. My parents liked him and even though they didn't have a lot of extra to go around, he was a frequent guest for dinner with my parents. In fact, he would come over on his own and sip on tea with my mother. They were both from aristocratic backgrounds and seemed to connect in a special way. As for him and me, I think there was mutual comfort in being outsiders. I worked on Bart's campaign when he ran for student union president, which he won. I guess my skills as a campaign manager were better than as a candidate. However, there was a challenge to the election and eventually Bart was defeated on a recount and technicalities. The challenge to the results came with accusations of racism. Bart went on to a career in academia, where he did a PhD on Rosa Luxemburg's understanding of Marx, followed by a rich career in the civil service working on human rights- and racism-related issues.

The last two years at university were just fantastic. I was on the honour role. I wound up getting credit for organizing conferences. Lloyd Axworthy was my political science professor and he talked about Martin Luther King Jr. and Selma, Alabama. He opened up the world to us. This was the early to mid-sixties and so much was going on to learn about. Later on, as an activist, I would oppose Axworthy on many issues. I took part in a public debate with him in 1970 where he supported Trudeau's implementation of the *War*

Measures Act. In that debate, I read the FLQ (Front de libération du Québec) manifesto publicly because the University of Winnipeg student newspaper, *The Uniter*, had published 1500 copies in their run and then, because the police claimed the students were publishing sedition, the *Uniter* staff went around and gathered up the paper so people couldn't read it. While the police were saying the manifesto was seditious, in fact, it was a plain and simple justice issue and the police and the government were preventing the public, even the freethinking university public, from hearing one side of the argument. They were preventing a Marxist critique of the socio-economic system that produced great injustices and inequalities in Quebec. We organized a march that gathered five hundred people to walk from the World War II cenotaph on Memorial Boulevard to the Richardson Building on Portage Avenue, about seven blocks away. Having known the experience of vanquished liberties in Europe, I was not going to stand for it in Canada.

I was a Liberal, a member of the Young Liberals in 1965 and 1966, and then I joined the New Democratic Youth of Canada's Manitoba chapter, the Manitoba Young New Democrats (MYND), because a German friend recruited me. At that time, however, I was no great radical. I was excited to learn and to meet new people.

The Young Liberals had our first demonstration with a professor, a Quaker who was not allowed to come into Canada because he preached free love and the right of communists to speak on campuses. His name was Milford Q. Sibley and we organized a bus to take twenty-five or thirty people out to the airport because he wasn't allowed to come into the country and was stuck there. We picketed and tried to show that this was unfair and unjust. He was made to fly back to Grand Forks that night but the decision was reversed and three weeks later he flew back and made his speaking engagements, no doubt much better attended for all the free advertising. That was my first protest! It was in March of 1965.

Within a year, I was involved in presenting a brief to the Minister of Immigration for Canada about this very issue with the Winnipeg Citizen's Committee on Immigration, an ad-hoc grassroots committee made up of activists from a variety of backgrounds including the "Voice of Women" [for Peace] (VOW), which still exists and remains active in the movement.

I wrote for the student newspaper and I was involved in model parliaments and model United Nations like I had been in high school, but I was much more committed. Tom Axworthy, Lloyd's brother, who went on to be an influential academic within the Liberal Party, recruited me to be in the model parliament. I was Minister of Immigration, while he was Prime Minister of Canada.

In 1967, when I was twenty-two, I took some time to go to Europe. I wanted to visit my relatives in Turkey and Greece and see my friend George Tillman, whom I had known from university, and who was living in Switzerland. I was also keen to see what Berlin looked like. I had ambitious plans. Using connections I made by spending time at the YMCA and following the suggestion of contacting the World Council of Churches, I began to write letters telling both organizations I had done work with youth and recreation. I started by taking the train to Montreal because Expo 67, the World's Fair, was on. From there I went to New York, where I stayed at Columbia University for three days, because I had a cheap flight through an Icelandic airline that was going to Luxemburg. This was back before jet engines — the flight took thirteen hours and I went immediately to a train all the way to Geneva, Switzerland!

That is where I met my friend and stayed a while before getting on another train, the Orient Express, which took three or four days and nights, to get me to Istanbul. I spent October and November with my aunt and her family. I spent my days drinking chai and eating lamb. I can still taste the lamb when I think of it. It was amazing. I also remember the bazaars. Nothing had a price. You could haggle for an hour over a bar of soap. Shopping for the day's food with my aunt seemed to take the entire day. I spoke German to my aunt and her husband, who, somewhat ironically, spoke English because he had been a prisoner of war in Canada. My other aunt, in Greece, was more comfortable with Russian so the trip was also an opportunity to keep up my languages.

There was a military dictatorship in Turkey and everything was strictly controlled. Even some photographs were considered illegal. I took a picture of the Sultan Ahmet Camii, known worldwide as the Blue Mosque, which had been a church at one time. Pictures taken inside were not allowed and at that time the military had power to arrest without question. It was a stunning building and I wanted a souvenir. I am glad I don't have a story to tell about the ten years I spent in a Turkish prison.

I had another aunt to stay with in Greece. At that time, Greece and

Turkey were far from friendly with each other and I remember there were only two passengers on the airplane to Greece. I was there about three weeks but got sick and spent quite a bit of the time recovering in bed. I heard there that some work with youth, under the direction of the church, had materialized for me in Berlin and I took the train from Athens through Austria and Munich all the way to Berlin. I arrived in Berlin late in November of 1967 just as the massive student upheavals were about to begin in Europe. Paris and Berlin were the two centres with the most activity. It was just chance that the work came up there, a matter of being at the right place at the right time to catch all that energy. I stayed seven months in Berlin until I came back to Canada in June of 1968.

Even though I had a passport saying I was born in Berlin, I was treated as a *gastarbeiter*, a guest worker. The Turkish and Greek stamps in my passport didn't help much either. The German authorities were, as you could imagine, a little nervous about all young people. The church I worked for had gotten me a couple of extensions, but ultimately they couldn't continue to arrange them for me, because the government didn't want foreigners working in Berlin. Turks were harassed constantly and were often taken to the police station to prove why they were needed as workers. They were never allowed to be citizens, they were never allowed to vote. Germany still has a "once a foreigner, always a foreigner" mentality. I called it a fascist system; even the church that I worked for had to play by the rules so I did appreciate their trying to get my work extensions.

I wound up working about six months for the church, and it was fun. I worked with a bunch of working-class kids. I introduced them to ten-pin bowling, miniature golf, movies and other things that were all there but they just had never done. I got in trouble for taking them to an anti-Vietnam War movie. I was working for the Lutheran Church, and one of the priests had a "better dead than red" attitude. I also rattled his cage by listening to rock music with the kids. You don't have to be a radical to be seen as one. Fortunately, the other priest I worked with the most had travelled in the United States and had been to Chicago, even meeting the American community activist Saul Alinsky. He was always on my side.

The student movement broke out in April of 1968. There were huge riots in Berlin, as elsewhere in Europe, with some people throwing Molotov cocktails and the police water-bombing the crowds. I was water-bombed at one demonstration. That water was anything but soft. Rudi Dutschke, who had been the leader of the Students for a Democratic Society (SDS) movement, had been shot by a right-wing student and it was at the demonstration protesting that shooting that I was water-bombed. That greatly affected me. The few demonstrations I had gone to in Canada had never made me feel indignant the way getting water-bombed did. I met Black Panthers there, marching at this demonstration, and got to know some of them. Most of them could speak English and that drew me in. The

On his way to being a radical

more progressive priests supported me, bringing together a teach-in at the church that centred on the war in Vietnam. The right-wing priest, who actually went on to serve in South Africa under Apartheid, accused me of supporting the Communist Party and distributing their propaganda, but I had done nothing of the sort.

On May Day 1968, I marched with fifteen thousand people to Kreutzburg, a working-class area in Berlin, for a peaceful demonstration. That march radicalized me. I saw police taking students who had probably nothing to do with the demonstration and beating them with clubs. My reaction was to want to meet militancy with militancy.

May Day has been important to me ever since. It saddens me that so few come out to commemorate the creation of the eight-hour work day. The workers of Chicago were working ten to fourteen hours a day in 1886 and 250,000 gathered in Haymarket Square to protest. Only guns and bombs could disperse them. Eight of the Haymarket activists were arrested, one of whom was sentenced to fifteen years in prison while the other seven were sentenced to death. Four of them were hanged, one killed himself in prison, and the other two had their sentences commuted to life in prison. Before the end of the century, marches were happening all over the world and continue until today. I spend the year looking forward to singing "The Internationale" on May Day.

There were teach-ins all over the place in Berlin at that time. Politics was part of every conversation. People were constantly talking. I never saw or experienced anything like it before or since. On every street corner people aged eight to eighty were talking, asking why the students were doing this, what was going on. Everybody was involved. Not that everyone was an activist, but they were all asking questions and talking. It was a city that cared about itself and what it was. The student demonstrations only lasted a week, but it was an unbelievable feeling. It was like an electric shock that wakes everybody up. And you're talking about a city of two million people. There wasn't anybody who didn't have an opinion about something or other, and cared about it.

Nothing in my forty plus years of activism felt like that week. My life-long frustration comes from knowing that kind of potential at a young age. I know people can be that alive. Those who have never experienced the power of a united, concentrated movement can't understand it in the same way as those of us who have.

I have enjoyed reading the work of some of the European radicals. *Obsolete Communism: The Left-Wing Alternative* by the anarchist Cohn-Bendit brothers is an important book from its time. The Cohn-Bendits are but two of many of the new left that became influential in the German Green Party. Dutschke, one of the most prominent spokespeople of the student movement in Germany in the 1960s, was published only in German and then only after being shot in the head in 1968. He died on Christmas Eve 1979 when he had a seizure in his bathtub.

I was given an opportunity to stay in Berlin when the Lutheran Church wanted me to work as a translator but I still would have been a *gastarbeiter*, meaning reapplying to stay every few months and being hassled by the police at each turn.

The church gave me some holidays, so I went to Prague. This was just weeks before the Russian invasion on August 20, 1968. It was called the "Dubček era" of so-called "humanist socialism," as the Czechs were defining themselves as unique from the Russians. So much was happening all over the world. The unrest continued in Europe. Robert Kennedy was shot, Martin Luther King Jr. was shot — these were heavy times. I met Czech students and they all suspected the Russians were going to invade. The hostility permeated everything but they all had questions for me. "What's going on? Why did Martin Luther King get assassinated? What's going on with the riots?" I had the role, the perfect role for a Canadian, of not belonging in any one camp but being able to talk to and relate to everyone. It was important for me to identify myself as a Canadian who spoke German. My Russian background would have made me *persona non grata* in Czechoslovakia.

Protests would happen spontaneously. A rumour came out that Cuba had been involved in the Kennedy assassination and the same day there were hundreds of students outside the Cuban embassy protesting. I was back in Canada when the invasion came, but there were protests in Berlin before I left and I read about them in German newspapers back in Winnipeg. They were anti-Stalin protests and were a different lot than those protesting the Vietnam War, as these European tensions meant so much more to the people in Berlin, more than the war. It was a heady time. You were kept busy just trying to understand the political changes that were tumbling all over the place.

Becoming a peace activist seemed a natural thing. I had the childhood experience of the ravages of war and the teenage experience of the kind of bigotry that fuels war. To that, I added my brief but educational "inside" experience of the military followed first by some passionate and brilliant professors and then being in the very middle of the student movements in Europe. When I came back to Canada, I was able to bring all these experiences together with other progressives. I am a designer peace activist.

3

Running for Mayor

"When someone asks me what I have done with my life, I have an answer: I got involved in the running of our city."

I first entered politics in 1971 when I sought and lost the NDP nomination for city council. I had a very active role in the NDP when I joined the New Democratic Youth (NDY) after a demonstration in 1970. I was still under the age of thirty and therefore very welcome in the NDY; I was on provincial council because the NDY had a seat at the table. The NDY appointed me; I wasn't elected to that position.

I was involved in policy making by the provincial government. I would go to various meetings and would challenge cabinet ministers. They were there and they held power, so I challenged them on what they were doing. Sid Green especially didn't like me, and Joe Borowski certainly didn't like me, but I wasn't going to those meetings to be liked. One of the big issues was amalgamation: several municipalities (including Winnipeg, St. James, St. Boniface and nine others) would become the City of Winnipeg and what came to be called Unicity. There was a committee headed by Lloyd Stinson, who had been the leader of the CCF (Co-operative Commonwealth Federation) in the early sixties. I was critical of some parts of Unicity, although I was supportive of others. Stinson was asked to chair the committee that would be involved in the municipal elections of 1971 and I, as a NDY representative, was elected to this committee. They charged me with recruiting civic candidates to run for the NDP in 1971.

They decided not to run a candidate for mayor, which I thought was a mistake. They ran thirty-nine candidates and I was going to run in one of the constituencies. Then Winnipeg's labour movement decided that they wanted to run a candidate in the constituency that I chose. With a lot of pressure on me, I gave up my nomination. I had worked hard; I had gotten people to nominate me. In fact, Sid Green's sons, Arthur and Martin, were very involved in pushing to nominate a Labour candidate. Stinson's book,

Political Warriors, is an excellent source for getting a flavour of those days and the ways in which socialist politics were playing out. The binding is shot on my own personal copy. We had some good internal discussions about policy, including police oversight, promoting community media, connecting ourselves to the Waffle movement and consumer education. We were pushing the edges of what politics in city hall was normally about.

In 1974, I ran in the core area, the Ross House ward, and lost badly, although I was third of six candidates. I didn't expect to win but there had been a split within the NDP municipal organizations and the Civic Reform Coalition (CRC) had been formed, which was like an alternative to the NDP. I ran on behalf of the CRC. I had run for chair of the CRC but Evelyn Shapiro won. Evelyn was a social work professor at the University of Manitoba and has the legacy of being the person who introduced "home care" to Manitoba. The CRC ran a number of strong candidates, but of them, only Evelyne Reese, running in the St. Boniface ward, managed to win because she was so involved and well known in St. Boniface. Later she ran provincially for the Liberals.

The CRC had a cohesive mandate that allowed both liberals and radicals to feel comfortable. We wanted the Resident Advisory Groups (RAGs) — groups of residents as big as twenty who would meet regularly to both bring concerns from the community to a councillor and provide feedback on what council was doing — to be expanded and given more authority. We got on board with Mayor Glen Murray's "New Deal" way of thinking, to improve revenue streams from provincial and federal government to cities. We raised issues of relocating the Canadian Pacific Railway (CPR) rail lines out of the inner city and considering the environment when implementing transit plans. We wanted to move responsibility for welfare to the province and develop a recreational river walk. Running as a Labour Election Committee candidate for the school board, Joe Zuken was the key "face" of the socialist left. Brenda Dineen, mayoral candidate for the League for Socialist Action, came second in the race, being beat out by incumbent Stephen Juba. The political discussions were extensive, and involved people from different groups and parties. Many of the ideas put forward by the CRC were realized.

My running for the CRC while I was still a member of the NDP was frowned upon, but I had an active campaign. Ken Wong, a conservative, won the ward. He is still around, doing business in town. James Campbell ran for the NDP and finished a distant second. Violet Stoppel ran as a "welfare candidate" and I liked the fact that she highlighted the right of welfare recipients to participate in politics as candidates. I took some steps towards a class action suit after that election to take on the provincial government on behalf of all voters. I wanted to get financing from business and unions stopped because it undercut democracy. When someone had a big union or big business behind them they could steamroll through an election. Thirty-five years later, in 2009, the NDP government finally passed a bill preventing those very donations, just nicely timed with my retirement. A few of my losses became wins for other people.

Brenda Dineen was a 26-year-old when she ran for mayor in 1974, supported by the Winnipeg League for Socialist Action (WLSA). She garnered six percent of the vote. I was involved in helping her the following April when a man going by the name of "Chris Mathieson," who attended WLSA events, was identified as Christie Brian Rush, a Winnipeg police officer. He drew attention to himself when he not-so-smoothly tried to steal a WLSA signup sheet with all the contact names on it. It was Winnipeg's little echo of the Watergate scandal. The city minimized any involvement and, even in the heady days of the 1970s, this gross violation of privacy failed to gain traction. Brenda moved to Vancouver shortly after this came out.

I also ran in 1975 in a by-election. I ran in Wolseley as I was living there. Frank Johnson, a lawyer who ran as an Independent, won. Jim Maloway (NDP) came second and then moved on to be a MLA in Elmwood. Werner Goetze, a porter for the CPR and a dear friend, ran as a Libertarian and finished behind me.

In 1977, I decided to run for both council and mayor, which they allowed at the time. If I ever had delusions of electoral success, they were gone at the end of this campaign. After 1977, losing never bothered me anymore. After 1977, there was a completely different purpose for me in running for political office. I rarely got support from anybody on the left because the left never took civic politics seriously enough. Liberals cared more about urban issues than radicals did. The radicals focused more on provincial and federal issues. I had all kinds of individuals who would support me because I had fought for the welfare rights groups, but these people generally were poor and difficult to mobilize into a campaign team.

In 1977, more than one hundred people told me that the only reason they voted was that I was on the ballot. They said, "If you're not on the ballot, we don't bother voting." That was my reason for running every time until 2002! I am a firm believer in democracy and a central part of true democracy is having real choices.

On average, about a hundred people phoned me each election. Some gave me money and others offered their support in other ways. I felt I owed it to those hundred people. Most of the left never understood why I ran. They just let me be. Many people in the left never voted. I don't think many members

Getting his papers in order for his first run at mayor

of the Communist Party ever endorsed or supported me. Individual communists did, but I know the Communist Party supported all kinds of other candidates.

Personally, I supported Greg Selinger when he ran for mayor in 1992 and I supported Glen Murray in 1998, because I, and many others on the progressive left, thought he would be progressive. I supported Joe Zuken in his run for mayor in 1979. Bill Norrie hammered Joe Zuken by about 80,000 votes. The *New York Times* came to Winnipeg to interview Zuken because they thought this could be the first communist ever to be elected mayor of a North American city. It could have been quite something. He always did very well in his own ward because he was a great worker for his constituents, not because there was a groundswell of support for his communist ideals. He was productive, though. The existence of kindergarten in our city and province can be traced back to him. I generally agreed with him, but we were totally opposed to each other on the Sherbrook-MacGregor overpass. He was for it; I was against it. Joe thought the overpass could connect the North End with downtown, but I thought there were ways to accomplish this without the expropriation and dismantling of a neighbourhood. We weren't socially connected but he liked the links I could make.

I was connected to the NDP and he wasn't, so he made a habit of probing me for the latest happenings. I guess you could say I was his spy in the NDP. He was bright and tireless; there are good reasons he was successful and so respected. I was quite happy to run in a by-election rather than run against him. His running became international news and Peter Warren, the host of CJOB's Action Line, was threatened enough to put out a scare campaign.

I also supported two Métis candidates who were elected to city council in 1971. In fact, they were the first two Métis ever to be elected. One was George Munroe, who was director of the Indian and Métis Friendship Centre. He was a militant Aboriginal who was very close to the American Indian Movement at that time. I helped him a lot and we still keep in touch, even though he eventually became a Liberal, running unsuccessfully in a provincial election against Eric Robinson in Ruperstland. I also worked on Lawrie Cherniack's campaign. Lawrie was a city councillor from 1971 to 1974. He went on to an important career as a labour lawyer. His father was Minister of Finance in Schreyer's government. He raised the issues that needed to be raised and had the credibility to win elections, a combination I never seemed to be able to put together. I also supported Cyril Keeper in 1977, who is a long-time Manitoba Métis politician and still a very close friend of mine. He went on to become a federal MP for the NDP from 1980–1988.

In 1977, I gained 5682 votes. It was my best showing for mayor but issues are always more important than votes. I ran on all kinds of issues including welfare reform, urban sprawl, expropriation, housing and welfare rights. I take the vote total as a sign of my higher public profile, meaning some people had to be hearing the issues I was raising. I gained a certain amount of respect in that campaign because I didn't spend very much money. I had no money, actually. I was unemployed at the time, and one of the issues that came up was that I was on unemployment insurance. Unemployment insurance decided to cut me off saying that I was not looking for work. I responded by arguing that, "Running for mayor is looking for work because if I get elected, I get paid!" The public interest lawyer, Arne Peltz, decided to take my case. We went to the Appeal Commission of the Unemployment Insurance Commission, and we won! In fact, I helped a couple of other candidates who had been on unemployment insurance when they were running for city council and were cut off. A two-to-one split decision viewed running for office as a legitimate effort to get a job. That got a lot of publicity too. I have to give Arne Peltz full credit for that one. He only represented me once and he came away with a victory. Still, it was a rough time. Because I had no money, I was earning only $104 weekly on my unemployment insurance payments and, on top of that, my daughter was born around that time, in 1976. Trying to sort out with her mother how we would care for her was very difficult, even considering my entire campaign budget was less than $150. Having to fight in these hearings for my basic sustenance did not make it any easier for us.

Bev Smith and I lived together from the seventies until the early eighties when she moved to Montreal with our daughter and stayed there. Bev and I were never married as neither one of us were particularly committed to the institution and at the time open relationships were common. For me, the open nature of our relationship was more about allowing me to stay fully committed to my work and politics, which always came first. To picture my life in the seventies and eighties is to picture a very non-traditional family that lived in poverty and struggled to get by. Bev and I shared similar political views and some would even say that she is to the left of me, as she often told me that my participation in elections gave legitimacy to a corrupt system. Bev has been in Montreal since her move in 1983 and we remain good friends and talk regularly on the phone. Even just after she moved, she was very cooperative in helping me stay in touch with our daughter, Tegan, over the phone and helped to have her come to Winnipeg to spend summers with me as she grew up.

I was part of the Winnipeg Citizens' Movement, a group similar to the CRC that ran candidates in municipal elections, in 1977. Pete Hudson and Evelyn Shapiro were co-chairs. We tried to elect a progressive council. In 1977, it was clear that I was running as a socialist candidate. Since the NDP was not running anyone, this was a campaign between Robert Steen, a Tory MLA, and Bill Norrie. They ran remarkably similar campaigns. Stephen Juba, the incumbent mayor, dropped out late in the day after everyone had assumed he would run again. It was clear to us that he had done this intentionally because he didn't want Bernie Wolfe, a long-time city councillor and well known in Winnipeg, to run with a chance of winning. There was a lot of bad blood between Bernie Wolfe and Steve Juba, but it is probably better that Bernie Wolfe tells this story than me. It was too late for Bernie

Wolfe to run when Juba dropped out, so Bernie Wolfe never became mayor of Winnipeg, which was his great ambition. Had Bernie run and won in 1977, our city might look very different now. He had the unique ability to relate to and have the respect of politicians of all stripes even though he was, perhaps without the name, a conservative. Some call him "the best mayor we never had."

Bill Norrie's first and only defeat was in that election. Steen, who was a Red Tory, probably would have changed city hall had he had the chance, but he died a year later. He had liver cancer and he was only forty-five years old. I had a community television program going at the time, and he promised me that once he won, if he won, I would be the first one to interview him. I wound up having a whole hour-long show after his victory. When he passed away, I sent a tape of the show to his family and they sent me a very nice thank-you letter. Having all the media in the studio to watch me do the interviewing was a twist on the usual story. I have spent my life on the edges, but Steen brought me right to centre stage. Norrie won the by-election of 1979, and he never lost any elections after that. I supported Zuken in that election and he came second with 24,650 votes. Norrie won and then he won again and again, until he retired. I ran for city council in the 1979 by-election in the Tache ward posing the question, "Do you want the ICEC [Independent Citizen's Election Committee] Developer's Dream, which turns out to be the People's Nightmare?" Housing was a key issue in the ward, so that is where a lot of my effort went.

In 1983, after relocating to Calgary in the hopes that my job prospects would be better there, I ran for Calgary City Council. I had printed posters and was set for a run for mayor when some community workers told me not to run. They were vague about why but made it clear I was not to run. This was Ralph Klein's first run at the job and perhaps they felt beholden to him for some reason. They eventually offered to pay me to run for council in Ward 8 where I lived, $100 up front and $400 afterwards. This covered my entry fee and printing costs. Then, they followed me around to make sure I did what they asked and, after the election, they said they didn't want to pay me the $400 but, since we had all signed a contract, they eventually did pay. I ended up getting just as much press for running for council as I would have running for mayor because socialism just wasn't on the radar in Calgary. If you had followed me around every day of my life, this is the one time where I am open to the accusation of being crooked. I took $500 to run for council rather than mayor because the few people who I thought might have supported me wouldn't do so unless I ran only for council. This is my entire history of being "on the take" and you have to know that a lot of people did a lot better than me at that game. I am still connected with those community workers; however I will never know why they thought it was worth their while to do that — it's not like I was going to steal votes from Klein.

I was Calgary's John F. Kennedy, synonymous with anything on the left. Many Calgarians liked my slogan "Concrete Jungle or Green Space" which offered the view that the recession gave the city a moment to breathe and actually think about how it developed itself. Klein had the image of being a populist unfettered by ideology. However, he was a right-winger, plain and simple, and I used my campaign every day to try and undermine the myth he presented. I raised a wide variety of issues including the call for a city referendum that would declare Calgary a nuclear-free city and seek the banning of cruise missile testing in northern Alberta. Back then, the missiles were presented as not having "first strike" capability but we all found out otherwise a few years later on the first day of the Gulf War. Another issue outside of the transportation, housing, recreation and income issues that I always raised was the Saddledome, the hockey arena. There had been huge cost overruns in its construction and nobody seemed to care. I called for a public judicial inquiry.

When I came back from Calgary, I enrolled in courses in social work at the University of Manitoba. There were nothing but fights. I got involved with all these left-leaning professors. Some of them were ex-communists. In fact, one of them was the son of the leader of the Polish Communist Party here in Winnipeg during the 1930s and 1940s, Len Kaminski. There were several of us in this cohort who were older than the average student. I was forty-one. We would challenge the professors because we all had life experience that they didn't have. I wasn't scared. Am I going to let the professor intimidate me? If I was hearing bullshit, I would say so and most professors didn't like to be challenged. Their power base usually served them well. I was thrown out of one of the classes, literally. Two women walked out with me, they were feminists. The professor was a Marxist. Many women didn't think in the left-right, Marxist-conservative political ideology so prevalent in those days, so they would get impatient with him and his lack of sensitivity to what was going on. My favourite topic was ideology and I didn't like the way he was handling it, so I got angry and spoke up. In response, he tried to fail me, but for the exam I studied the hardest I ever had in my life. I have terrible handwriting so I always print. This was a two-hour exam, which is a long time to print. I printed two and a half exam books on Marxist theory and I got forty-six out of fifty, the highest mark of all the students, and he was angry — actually mad as hell! Somebody else, not him, had marked the paper.

I made a formal complaint to the University against him for harassing women and for general disrespect. Nothing ever happened, but I went to the Dean and made sure the complaints were heard. Ultimately, I got a B or B- in his class. He had tried to get me down to a C-. He told me that I was one day late in submitting an assignment of an analysis of Milton Friedman, the most conservative of neo-conservative economists there was. I said, "Never again am I going to go back to university, and these people are nuts." I didn't have work and the student loans helped me eat, but it was a very rough year because my father was very ill and I was taking care of him. I was pulled in a lot of directions as this was in the run-up for the 1986 election for mayor. I made quite a reputation for myself on campus and I believe I actually created enough stir there that the professor wound up changing his behaviour. He and I actually talk to each other these days. We speak somewhat civilly, although I couldn't stand him for many, many years. I believe that he's retired now and working on promoting history in the North End and I don't think of him as a sexist anymore.

There were several great opportunities during the time I studied social work. I heard Bishop Remi De Roo speak about "God's preferential option for the poor" and "emerging liberation theologies" at a Networking for Needs conference held at Immaculate Conception Church. These ideas were all new to me.

In the 1986 Winnipeg mayoralty election, I received over 3000 votes and placed fourth. I was in the peace movement and I had organized the Urban Resource Centre, and I had started writing again. But, I was moving towards the Greens, and introducing what I called green ecological ideas into city politics. I took my lead from the German Greens. While I have been credited with introducing the Green Party to Winnipeg, technically, this is not true. I had connections to early newspapers like *The Green*, *Ecospeak* and *Pollution Probe* and I was the first to introduce Green concepts to a municipal election, but there was no party involved. Yet, I am comfortable saying that I brought their ideas onto Winnipeg's political landscape.

The whole notion of environmental protection and sustainability in terms of urban planning was not in the conversation even in 1989. I was treated as a significant candidate because I raised the whole issue of how we live and whether or not we can sustain ourselves. I always spoke of the Green movement rather than of a party with the structure and other trappings that prevent the organic growth of the movement. This issue has remained in the party, as younger members are more interested in promoting the ideas within a movement than the more pedantic work of building an election machine. Others in the movement are much more academically inclined and I had the privilege of meeting several of them when I was asked to coordinate presentations for the Socialist Studies Society at the Learned Societies Conference in Laval, Quebec, in June 1989. We called it the "Red-Green Movement in Canada" and presentations were made by Eric Darier, a political scientist from McGill, Jennifer Sells, an eco-feminist from Trent, and others from across the country. I wonder if Steve Smith had read through my articles and had the name for his successful "Red-Green" TV character (from 1991–2006) jump out at him?

Being able to read German helped me follow what was going on with the Greens in West Germany. I used the slogans, "Not to the left, not to the right, but in front!" and "Don't Agonize … Organize!" My friend Kent Gerecke, professor of city planning at the University of Manitoba, was also very active in sharing the vision of social ecology, which goes far beyond a single issue like animal rights that many people still think of when they think of the Green movement. Social ecology is a broad-reaching view that begins with a critique of society's hierarchical structure. In 1996 the Green Party of Canada was finally established in Manitoba, becoming the Green Party of Manitoba two years later. I was involved with Marcus Buchart and others in early meetings that went back as far as 1988, but my energy was more for the broader movement than developing party structure.

I have voted Green but I have never been a member of any Green party other than the left caucus of an international Green organization that operated out of Chicago. That was where I came to know the work of Murray Bookchin, who offered a coherent vision for the Green movement in urban politics, an area ignored by most Greens, who thought efforts were best spent at the federal level. *The Ecology of Freedom* and other writings by Bookchin were a big influence on the German Greens; *Ecology* helped me bring together a lot of my own thinking. His ideas were the blueprint for my Green campaigns. He was a true visionary in the way he brought together varying streams of thought such as libertarianism, socialism and anarchism. He offered a counter voice to the deep ecology movement in calling for involvement in municipal life, be it in a city, town or village. He died at the age of eighty-five in 2006 and was busy writing and speaking until his very last days. I never actually met him but my friend Ken Gereke went to courses presented by him in Vermont and spoke with deep appreciation for his substance and power. When I hear a phrase like "progressive centrist" in relation to the Green Party, I dismiss it; the phrase is an oxymoron. By definition, centrists are conservative, not wanting to take risks or progress with any real change.

Russell Doern finished a strong second in the 1986 election for mayor, behind Bill Norrie. He had been a NDP cabinet minister and a great supporter of Ed Schreyer as premier, but eventually left the party because of its pro-bilingualism stance and some other issues. He ran as an Independent provincially in 1986 and, after losing, offered his name for mayor. We had both left the NDP but for different reasons and I moved to the left while he moved to the right, so we had lots to debate during that election.

Peter Juba came a distant third, based on the strength of his last name alone. He was not much of a politician and his showing made a sad statement about democracy when many of those who voted thought they were voting for Steve Juba — Winnipeg's mayor from 1957 to 1977 — and the two of them were, perhaps, not related at all. (Peter Juba claimed not to know himself if he was related to Steve Juba.) There were ten candidates that year. Allen Bleich, who now works with the Canadian Union of Public Employees (CUPE), ran with some anarchist ideas and had a Rhinoceros Party approach, mocking the entire process. He represented the Very Independent Citizen's Election Committee (VICE) and used the name Bill Lingual, the son of Uni and Multi Lingual. He said his budget for the entire election was five bucks! He placed seventh, with three candidates behind him. I like what he did. He is a funny man and he does good work for the unions.

In 1988 I ran in a by-election in the Glenlawn ward. Al Golden won out against seven of us. As usual, that campaign gave me opportunity to raise the issues of affordable housing, welfare rights, rapid transit, urban sprawl and other matters important for working people. Marshall Hughes was the official agent for the "Green Reform Committee," which was represented by me and by Willie Kurtz in the University ward. Willie is an owner of Humboldt's Legacy, a store in Wolseley that specializes in environmentally friendly and politically sensitive products. He has taken the values he brought into products and expressed them to an entire generation through his business. Many businesses like his have not been able to sustain themselves. It is a testimony to Willie's character that he continues to do so well in offering a true alternative to big box shopping.

In 1989, Bill Norrie won handily but I received my highest vote ever, coming in third with 6,865, beating out Conrad Santos, the highest profile NDPer in the race. Norrie didn't even run a campaign. He didn't have to. He beat the number two person, J. Frank Syms, by over 70,000 votes. Syms had been, at one point, the president of the provincial New Democrats, but had become a conservative in everything but name by the time he ran for mayor. It was a farce of an election and I think people were insulted that it was such a foregone conclusion. My numbers probably reflect the parking of protest voices as much as any real commitment to the ideas I spoke of throughout the campaign. Once again, I was pushing the Green agenda and I worked with Willie Kurtz and others who were ready to give themselves over to these issues. We tried to build a platform but as I was taking care of my father, who was quite sick at the time, and there being so few of us, forming a party with a full platform wasn't within our reach.

Some of the Green voices were anti-left in some ways and I didn't have the patience to be compromising with some of the views that were being put forward. I wouldn't speak now the way I did then. There were several local feature stories about me and about the Greens because they had some members elected to the German parliament in 1983 and they were more of a story than Norrie's non-campaign. I tracked down the history of the German Greens all the way to the "new left" when Germans were protesting the war in Vietnam. Many of the people who joined the Green movement in the mid-eighties stuck with the movement. There had been a similar surge of the Green movement in the U.S., but it retreated to almost nothing. I made a presentation in Chicago and said that the German Green movement that came out of 1979 was a continuation of the new left, and it laid the foundation to become a major political party by winning seats in 1983. Ultimately, the German Green movement betrayed itself by going into a partnership with the Social Democrats. They got into government but sacrificed too much to do so. In Winnipeg, we were not a party but we did like the environmental stands of a number of candidates for council and we endorsed eight candidates. Not all of them wanted to be endorsed by us, and Roger Young in particular, who ran in the Pembina-Riverview area, maximized the distance between the two of us.

I was able to put forth a number of my priorities with the attention that came to me in the press, at debates and other forums. I spoke about improving community with the decentralization of municipal government, more humanistic policies in the area of housing and challenging the corporate influence in the running of the city. I called for more community involvement from grassroots groups and for non-profit organizations to take control of some of the services that were provided by the city. I talked about more bicycle paths, an environmentally friendly electrified transit system, a better recycling system and a total restructuring of the city's tax system. I am still talking about these issues.

Seventeen candidates ran for mayor in the 1992 election. I worked for Greg Selinger, who is now premier of Manitoba. He ran a very respectable second. Susan Thompson had a lot more money and ran a campaign heavy with television ads that Greg couldn't match. With a week to go before the e-day, many thought he was going to win. Peter Warren gloated in an editorial that the election was a watershed because it was the "first time since the 1930s [that] no member of the Communist Party will be serving as an MLA, city councillor or school trustee," naming Irene Haigh as "the last Commie" to go down. This did not mean I was not able to raise the issues that I always brought to the table. The structure and ways of council, protecting the environment, removing education taxes from property taxes and holistic development were all front and centre in my campaign.

I didn't run for council in 1992. I ran a Green campaign for Winnipeg School Division Board in a ward that covered Wolseley and River Heights. This was hardly my base and I finished last with fewer than four percent of the vote. I was prevented from running in the municipal election because I had not turned in an audited statement of my expenses from the previous election. I couldn't afford the audit; it cost more than my campaign. It was too stupid a rule to adhere to, so I suffered the consequences by running for school trustee instead and that was certainly less work than running for mayor.

If I was a socialist in 1977 and a green in 1986, I was an anarchist in 1995. John Parry, who had been an NDP mayor in Sioux Lookout, talked about running for mayor on the left but never offered his name. I probably would have run again, even though I knew him, because it was the breadth of issues, not the win, that motivated me. I rehabbed the idea of "happenings" from the sixties. My campaign team consisted of myself, my good friend Willy Sheard and Lloyd Lawrence, who was a graduate student at the time. Lloyd has a very solid life as a CUPE organizer since those days.

I got a lot of press for being involved in the panhandling issue during the 1992 election, as I became a panhandler. I dressed like a panhandler and acted the part throughout the election. We fought a by-law that was to "deal with the whole issue." I was the first one to take it on and the press loved the guerrilla theatre method I used. It wasn't until the next election, though, in 1998, when Glen Murray, who was mayor at the time, actually listened to some extent, and city council asked the social planning council to lead a task force on the issue of the "squeegee kids" who were panhandling while washing windows at intersections. I was part of that debate, one of the few times in my political career where I felt I had a full voice and that others were listening to me. The report was great and was read across the country, but very few of the recommendations were ever implemented in Winnipeg.

The panhandling by-law, as it now stands, penalizes behaviour such as obstructing or impeding a person in the street for money, and does nothing to deal with the factors that may lead a person to panhandle, such as poverty, homelessness and/or a lack of education. The laws also ignore the racial components of the issue. Many of the panhandlers that business owners complain about in the Exchange District are Aboriginal and we are far past the time to face that reality. There are massive influxes of Aboriginal people from reserves who move to the city with very little urban experience and an understanding of urban living that differs radically from what they find. While more and more Aboriginal people are successful, many still face dire circumstances complicated by poverty and racism. Help is hard to find when they flee the poverty of the reserve. The panhandling by-law is also unenforceable. Very few citations have been given, and judges have not been interested in dealing with them either. We don't need a panhandling by-law. If someone is asking for money in an overly aggressive or violent way then that person should be charged with harassment or assault. Our unenforceable by-law is only a pretend solution. In Ottawa, the city let the local chapter of the Industrial Workers of the World (also known as the Wobblies) manage a licensing system for buskers, which has also been an issue Winnipeg has failed to resolve.

I also tried to push the issue of leadership and vision in the mayor's office during the 1992 election, as I saw Winnipeg as just sitting back and accepting the province's indifference to our revenue and responding too quickly to any kind of initiative put forth by the business community rather than having a plan for the health and wealth of our city. I talked about the problems with having school boards raise their money through property taxes and it finally looked, in 2012, as if something was going to happen in that area. At that point, some of the business leaders were talking about a new arena at the Forks site and I was opposed to that. Every chance I had, I kept the debate broad and introduced the basic idea that capitalism does not meet the social needs of the poor and spoke to those issues from that perspective rather than the "trickle down" kind of blather that comes from the business-supported candidates.

Ironically, given my last few years, I used the image of cancer in my 1995 campaign. I spoke of the city being organic, like a growing cell. Cities can either grow like a cancer, resulting in an unhealthy make-up of steel, concrete and mortar, or cities can be composed of an interaction of politics, culture, economics and the environment and be a healthy, liveable place identified by its people, not its physical structures. I surely wasn't the only one raising the issues of the weakening infrastructure at that time. Now, under Mayor Sam Katz, these problems have reached epic proportions and yet he wins his elections with a majority. It is an "out of sight, out of mind" mentality. As usual, I had to do what I could to get the press to listen to the issues that I thought were important. Thanksgiving was just a few weeks before the election and the coalition I was part of, called Food Not Bombs, put on a Thanksgiving meal in an abandoned house on Balmoral Street. The event put a face on poverty as the press shared the stories of how the people who were there found themselves in such poverty. We served vegetarian food to push the Green agenda and, by using an abandoned building, we talked about the need for social housing for the poor and needy. We used the kitchen in the house where I lived to make the meals, leaving our house smelling of borsht for several days.

I remember a student at the meal embarrassing Minister of Family Services Bonnie Mitchelson by talking to the press about the resentment he felt on learning of Mitchelson's $3,600 meal bill while hosting visiting ministers to Winnipeg while so many were starving on the streets. Adequate housing is the absolute basis of building a stable and productive life and, again, this was 1995 and only in 2010 did we start a clinical trial study of a "housing first" project in Winnipeg.

City police arrested me for but never formally charged me with break-and-enter for entering the Balmoral house, which the city had taken over for non-payment of taxes. At the same time, over at the Forks, fifty residents of Pukatawagan were protesting the lack of housing for single women and their children on their reserve. They made the trek from the Forks, where they were camped, to Balmoral Street and joined us. It was a very success-ful event. I don't think the Attorney General wanted to give me all the free newspaper coverage. I imagine the police were none too happy having wasted their time taking me to the Public Safety Building and booking me. The police were polite and perfunctory. Emily picked me up and we were given a heroes' welcome when we returned and joined the Food Not Bombs people for dinner.

Earlier in the 1992 election I had twice tried to get arrested. I started panhandling outside the Royal Bank building on Portage Avenue at Fort Street. I had sent the police a letter to tell them what I would be doing. Arne Peltz was ready to challenge the by-law in court under the *Charter of Rights and Freedoms*. The police said, quite simply, "Nobody complained." I guess, on this one, they were wise to me, and didn't want to give me the free public-ity. The press liked the story but we did not get our day in court. I made it clear that the by-law was not going to be enforceable and, as such, was just a big waste of time and money. This is exactly what it turned out to be. It did not end the issue of panhandling. Until we deal with the root issues of poverty, people will be forced to do what they need to in order to survive. Panhandling, as long as it is not aggressive or threatening, is protected as a right of freedom of speech.

I also led a number of people to jaywalk across Portage and Main, Winnipeg's famous intersection. For years, pedestrians have been forced to cross the street underground because the street is "guarded" by concrete barriers. The jaywalkers climbed over those chunks of concrete to protest their existence. Again, the police were not going to provide me with free publicity. They let us be.

The "barricades," as I like to call them, went up in 1979 and many people over the years have protested those silly walls. I remember disability activist Jim Derksen and Joe Zuken being among the first. I have been involved more often than I can remember in efforts to bring about change at the intersection, and each time I have mentioned that I do it as a tribute to Joe Zuken, who was so bothered by them. I still think of Joe when I am down there. When Susan Thompson was mayor, Jim Derksen and I had talks with her about removing the barriers and we were really going somewhere — we truly thought it was going to get done. But it has been many years since those talks and never again has it felt like we were going to get rid of them.

Theresa Ducharme, a long-time disability activist, was another candidate for mayor in 1995. She ran to raise issues related to people with disabilities. The Chamber of Commerce refused to invite Theresa and me to a debate at the Convention Centre but at least I was able to distribute some of my literature and ask a question before I was removed by security. The University of Winnipeg also had their security people give me a "cease and desist" order regarding campaigning on campus. I took these as victories. They wouldn't go so far if I wasn't a threat to them. It was an interesting campaign and I got a lot of press but I only garnered about half the votes I had in some other elections.

The lead-up to the 1995 election took a lot of time and energy, two meetings a week for seven months trying to respond to the issues related to all the visible poverty on our streets. Emily and I had been married for just two years. She was working full-time with the Manitoba League of Persons with Disabilities, and I had lots of free time to attend meetings and run errands. I would work an hour and a half in the morning delivering newspapers, and then I would work for an hour at lunchtime as a monitor at Laura Secord School and the rest of the day was mine, giving me lots of time for evening meetings and to get together during the afternoons or in the mornings.

I consider myself a professional radical. If I count all the demonstrations from 1968 until now, I cannot imagine anyone in Winnipeg who has been to more. I have participated in at least four hundred demonstrations. I was not the one who organized all of them, but I have been there to make my voice heard in Berlin, Ottawa, Toronto, Winnipeg, Calgary and other places. I have been master of ceremonies in at least a hundred out of those four hundred.

Some say, "Well, who cares? I mean, what has it accomplished?" When someone asks me what I have done with my life, I have an answer: I got involved in the running of our city. I went to thousands of meetings and joined countless organizations because there are issues that matter to people every day. I was on the board of directors of Legal Aid. Many of the paying jobs that I've worked have been political also. *Canadian Dimension* is a left-wing magazine, so I could push left-wing ideology when I worked there and there was no problem. I was head of the Winnipeg anti-poverty group when I was executive director of Neighbourhood Services Centre. At some level, they were all political. Running for office is part not only of what I have done but also who I am. For a year and half, in the early nineties, I had an administrative job with Ten Ten Sinclair Housing's Fokus housing units, which developed housing for people with disabilities. That was my first non-political employment.

When I lived in Calgary, I started at Hillhurst-Sunnyside Community Association while they waited for Peter Globensky to start as director. When he arrived, I shifted over to housing coordinator and did that until the funding ran out.

Delivering papers was fine, it is not political, but it was only for two hours in the morning. It was the *Winnipeg Sun*, and I was their employee of the month once. There wasn't really a down side. The papers would be late and customers would complain and occasionally I would come across a drunk coming home or a dog that was a little scary but generally it was a pleasant way to make some income. The *Winnipeg Sun* even chose me as "Carrier of the Year" in 2000. I also delivered flyers and *The Metro*. I see the irony in it as I probably disagree with just about everything they ever published, but you have to pay for the food you eat.

Most of the days delivering papers were much the same. Not many people were awake and you did the same houses each day. One incident does stick out in my memory: early one morning when I had Emily with me, it was storming real heavy. We got our car stuck on Denson Place in the West End and a retired schoolteacher named Stella Orisko was awake and came outside and shovelled with me for about twenty minutes. Then, after we got our car going, it ran out of gas. Orisko invited us in and fed us and let us have a nap while she dried our clothes. When the tow truck couldn't get through the storm, she called a friend who took us home, late in the afternoon, in his four-wheel-drive truck. He took as back to her house the next day, where she fed us again while we waited for the CAA tow truck to come and get our car. At the time, the *Winnipeg Free Press* had a "Random Act of Kindness" award and both Emily and I nominated her but she did not get it.

The lunch program at Laura Secord was also a non-political job. I supervised kids for an hour. I wasn't going to talk politics to the kids — I took care of them, and that's it. I enjoyed that work. My daughter, Tegan, had moved back from Montreal and had the job. I took it over for her when she went on a maternity leave. I stayed at that job for six years and eventually was seeing my own grandchildren at lunch every day. I had trouble with my cataracts and that led to me moving on from that job. I couldn't do the work because I couldn't see.

The last professional job I had was with *Canadian Dimension* in 1992. I just couldn't get a job with my reputation. That is why I have had to live off delivering newspapers, serving school kids lunch and the occasional freelance journalism job.

In 1998 I did not run for Mayor. I did not actually work for Glen Murray but I was hopeful for what he could bring and I signed his nomination papers. I had first met him when I was taking graduate school courses in social work at the University of Manitoba in the mid-1980s. He came to do a presentation on HIV/AIDS awareness and he was clearly very bright and able. A few years later, in 1989, when I met him when he was campaigning for a seat on city council, I had the same experience of thinking this guy knew what he was doing. As a city councillor, he was a hard worker and a smart voice. When he was mayor, I probably agreed with about ninety percent of his politics but thought his process was autocratic and secretive. He seemed to forget about those of us who supported him and didn't listen the way I thought he would. I wouldn't say he betrayed me personally, but politically, many of those who helped him get to the mayor's office were disappointed.

I ran, unsuccessfully, for the school board again in 1998. Again, I was not able to run for council due to the rules around financing. It is worse now. If you do not file an audited election expenses statement, the city takes you to court. It is undemocratic. It makes sense to me that if someone is elected that they should declare their backers to identify potential conflicts of interest, but this should not apply to those who are defeated and it just makes politics harder to get involved in. The rules are designed to prevent people like me doing the things I did, so it should be no surprise that this whole process still pisses me off!

I ran for mayor in 2002 against Glen Murray and received 2665 votes. People thought Glen was the best candidate with a chance to win and put their support behind him. I understand that. Again, I was there to keep the issues that I believe really matter on the table. Also, with a sense that Murray was a shoo-in to win, I spent my energy just trying to raise the democratic process, especially with young people. I opened my campaign with a press conference on Portage Avenue, explaining that "downtown Winnipeg is turning into a mini-Las Vegas, where gambling, prostitution and parties will only wreck the area." I explained how the True North Sports and Entertainment complex (now the MTS Centre) was the poster child for everything that is wrong with the city's approach to downtown revitalization. Instead of encouraging residents to move into the area, the new arena, big box developments and the tolerance of strip clubs and massage parlours will continue to pummel the vitality of the core of the city. I called it the "colonization" of downtown Winnipeg by corporate interests. Their interests are not for the well-being of the downtown but for their short-term profit. There is no magic connection. These interests of community well-being and corporations were and are at odds!

Another thrust of that election for me was the ongoing issue of scrapping the unenforceable anti-panhandling by-law and, instead, deal with the factors that may lead a person to panhandle, such as poverty, homelessness and a lack of education. I also campaigned for reform at city hall, as there was too much secrecy and the Executive Policy Committee had too much power. Glen Murray had campaigned in 1998 on changing the secretive culture, but in many ways it was worse with him than with Susan Thompson as mayor. As a councillor in October of 1997, Murray spoke strongly against the Cuff Report, in which consultant George Cuff recommended extending power to the mayor's office. Yet, as mayor, he exploited that report for all the power he could. I was scared as that election began that Murray would be seen as the obvious winner and, with several councillors facing acclamation, that we might have the lowest turnout ever. I feared a crisis of democracy.

As I have said earlier, I always had a handful of friends who offered to help and who gave me small donations, but in the 2002 election my friend Jeff Lowe took on the work of campaign manager and policy advisor. We are similar people with similar values and so he was easy to work with, but it was still helpful for another set of eyes and slightly different take on strategy and planning. Jeff moved to Winnipeg from New York via Toronto when I was in Calgary in 1983. Before we met, he had edited some of my writing for *City Magazine*. When I moved back to Winnipeg we worked together on the magazine and became friends. He was always supportive and remains a good friend and his help on that campaign was memorable. He knew I never wanted to go door-to-door but he would encourage me, saying that if people only knew me they would pay more attention to my ideas. I know this comes so easily, or at least appears to, for career politicians who will do whatever it takes to be elected, but by 2002 for sure, running for office again was the furthest goal I could imagine.

I had said before the 2002 election that it would be the last. Twenty campaigns were enough for anybody. Apparently, I am far short of the world record for number of elections lost. A Canadian, John C. Turmel, who ran mostly in Ontario as a Social Credit-leaning Independent, holds the world record for most elections lost: seventy-four. In Winnipeg, my closest competitor was Magnus Eliason, who persevered through thirteen elections before landing a seat on city council.

Mosquito fogging was also an issue in 2002 and I stood up for expanded larviciding and opposed the use of malathion. This was, of course, long before I developed my cancer, which I believe is due to that poison. Prior to the election, Mayor Murray had betrayed the community of Wolseley by promising not to fog and then going ahead and doing so anyway.

Since my retirement, I have supported Marianne Cerilli and Judy Wasylycia-Leis. They were both good candidates and both would have done a much better job than Sam Katz. Judy, in particular, took time to draw upon all the experience I had at city hall and to get my opinion on the issues facing the city.

In reality, looking at the political history of Winnipeg, no incumbent mayor has lost in a civic election since the 1930s. Regardless of whether the media proclaims you as a serious challenger or as a fringe candidate, the result will ultimately be incumbents and "also-rans."

Nick's last run for mayor of Winnipeg

Politics should be about what you stand for. Unfortunately, politics is all about winners and losers. Winnipeggers as a whole tend to be "small c" conservative, not interested in ideology whether it is left or right. They are more inclined towards pragmatism, asking questions about who can best fix roads and the infrastructure. It is because of this way of thinking we are ensured to face the continued tradition of mayors like Sam Katz.

In addition to my runs for mayor, I ran for NDP president ten times and tried to run for leader once. I was going to run against Schreyer after his first term in government and was pressured not to, because people said that it would look bad for a sitting premier to be opposed. I opposed him on many issues and running for leader was one way to get the voice of the left, and the roots of the party, on the table. In fact, they made sure I couldn't run by changing the rules and requiring signatures of twenty-five of the delegates in order to run. My desire to develop democracy in the NDP ended up in leading to the undermining of democracy. I ran for president every time I was a resident in the province and a member of the party, which added up to ten times between 1972 and 1986. I had also offered my name for leader in 1979 but eventually dropped out because I was content to support Muriel Smith, who ran with the support of the Waffle movement. She was a strong second to Howard Pawley, who won on the first ballot. I was particularly pleased to see her trounce Russell Doern, who placed third. I fared better with the

NDP presidential races than in my civic elections, often receiving more than twenty percent of the vote and coming second. The Manitoba NDP has been a centrist, capitalist-minded party since they were first elected. Running for president enabled me to keep the socialist agenda on the table as the party, getting the taste for power, drifted away from its roots. I was able to talk about the guaranteed annual income, full coverage for dental care, government control of mineral resources, rent controls, tenants unions, abortion rights, a thirty-hour work week and other issues in those 1970 campaigns. Some of these have been long since realized. Some are currently at risk and on others we have continually lost ground.

4

The Peace Movement

"There has been no period in human history where the voice for peace was not needed; this is certainly true in my life — the peace movement never ends."

I received my Bachelor of Arts Degree (Sociology) in October 1968 just after United College became the University of Winnipeg. I thought I had finished my studies in 1967, but I needed one science course to graduate, which I got through summer school. When Floyd Williston, manager of the Co-op Bookstore, heard I was around, he asked me to join the Winnipeg Committee for Peace in Vietnam — which then consisted of only a few people.

I had only been back from Europe for a couple of months and still had all that energy running through me. I was keen to be involved in any way I could. The Committee were planning their first major demonstration on October 26, 1968. That was the International Day of Protest Against the War in Vietnam. There was no structure to our group. Most members were liberals, but some communists were involved. They paid me a few hundred dollars from their own pockets to do some organizing. We got a thousand people out and I marched in the front. In those days, demonstrations were illegal unless you had the Canadian flag leading it. The professors and social workers wanted no part of the demonstration, but I did! I carried the flag proudly. That was my first picture ever in the newspaper — my first public appearance if you will. While I am thankful to live in Canada — without our health care system I wouldn't be alive — the idea that I was a flag-waving nationalist is still quite funny to me.

Around this time, I considered graduate school and sent letters and applications to various schools in Canada and in the U.S. One that accepted me was New Mexico State University in Las Cruces. I had to take the Graduate School Admissions Test. As I did not do very well, they rescinded their offer but encouraged me to take the test again. My heart wasn't in it. Many people I knew were going off to graduate school so it just seemed like the thing to

Nick was always a presence at Winnipeg's peace demonstrations

do. I certainly have no regrets, but if I had gone and spent three years in New Mexico at that point in my life, I imagine I would still be who I am, perhaps just in another place.

I was a member of the anti-Vietnam War movement through 1975, when the war ended. We had demonstrations every October. I was the organizer all those years but I was never paid again like I was the first year. Those demonstrations, and the anti-war movement, were a political minefield. In 1968, it was mostly liberals and communists; by 1970 the Trotskyists had moved into the peace movement and it became a battle between the Trotskyists on one side and the communists on the other. The liberals had pretty much left the organized part of the movement by then. The emerging Maoist movement made things even more complicated. Essentially, the peace activist group kept on being infiltrated; a change in focus, usually marked by a name change, would follow. The Trotskyist and Maoist influences were both calling for a violent response to the U.S. involvement in Southeast Asia, rather than for a cease-fire and peaceful resolution. Ken Kalturnyk was one of the Maoists. He has run as a Marxist-Leninist in five federal elections and has served the labour movement well since those days. Claire Culhane, a Quaker well known for her work and her prison reform writings, also supported our efforts.

The Ad-hoc Committee for the Mobilization of the International Day of Protest, to be held on November 15, 1969, was chaired by Ruth Pear. She was married to Ron Fletcher, a United Church minister, who moved on to Saskatchewan. We called him "Father Fletcher" because he was the only minister active with the NDY. Pear was just as active as her husband, but her life was cut short by cancer. Others involved in that work include some old-time communists like Mildred Lamb. Vern Gray, a social worker, and I were the only Independents in that we were not formally aligned either with the Trotskyists or the Communist Party. The Maoists never joined up with anyone. Vern became chair and I was the vice-chair because nobody would tolerate "the other side" in leadership.

Demonstration against cruise missile testing in Canada

There was more than just the Vietnam War to protest. It was a period of nuclear proliferation. The most memorable protest was when we circled the U.S. Consulate as part of an international day of protest on nuclear proliferation in September 1971. Both Howard Pawley, who was the municipal affairs minister at the time, and Mayor Stephen Juba were part of the demonstration denouncing the Americans for their weapon testing on Amchitka Island in Alaska. The tests went ahead but the fact that they allowed professors to cancel classes so students could attend protests on October 30, when the tests actually happened, provides a sense of the widespread opposition. There were protests across the country and even an attempted bombing of the consulate in Winnipeg. Mitchell Sharp, the Liberal Minister of Foreign Affairs, also spoke strongly against nuclear testing. We were anything but a fringe group on this issue.

There was little time for rest in between the end of the anti-Vietnam War work and the growing anti-nuclear movement. Between 1975 and 1979, many of us in the peace movement chose to devote our time to other social justice issues.

It was an incredible period after 1979 when the threat of nuclear war became a mainstream concern. Twenty-five thousand people marched in Winnipeg in 1982. I was in Calgary in 1982 when Howard Pawley, then premier, led that record crowd in protest against nuclear weaponry. He declared Winnipeg a nuclear-free zone, which a civic referendum supported. Many women, together with their children, came out, more than I had seen in the past. That may have been because they thought nuclear war was five minutes away, they would all be wiped from the earth and they didn't want their kids to die.

During the first Gulf War, we managed to attract two to three thousand people to two separate demonstrations in 1990 and 1991. Demonstrations during the Yugoslav wars brought out fewer people, but we did get seven or eight hundred out. The second invasion of Iraq produced a demonstration crowd in the spring of 2003 that was somewhere between five and seven thousand. That was the biggest demonstration I had ever been to in Winnipeg. It was also Carl Ridd's last demonstration. Carl was a relentless activist for social justice in Winnipeg for several decades. Along with working as a university professor and United Church minister, Carl was a Manitoba Sports Hall of Fame basketball star and a mentor to more people than seemed humanly possible. He died of cancer not long after the Iraq demonstration. Over the years, I came to know Carl, his wife Bev, their daughter Karen and the rest of their family. That is one impressive group in terms of living out their commitments. Carl was the one I had the privilege of knowing the best. I met him in the early seventies, when I was a student and he was teaching in the Religion and Culture Department at the University of Winnipeg. I never took classes with him but he was highly visible on campus and always had time for students. He became involved in the panhandling issue after talking to me and was a great voice. I will always remember his speech at that last rally in 2003. He was so articulate and so passionate; none of us knew he was sick. Maybe he didn't even know, but I expect that he did. I ended up with the same cancer specialist as he had.

Bruce McKay was another organizer I admired. He could run a meeting better than anyone I have ever met. He was open-minded but firm and focused. He planned well so it was clear that everyone involved knew what we were trying to do. He was an organizer for the Wobblies — the Industrial Workers of the World union — but I met him in several contexts. He loved the old labour songs and really kept the Wobbly tradition alive. In 2005, I received a labour movement award named after him for the work I had done on peace and social justice. It was a great honour to get an award with his name. He died at age fifty-six, just after Christmas in 2001, of a heart attack and, fittingly, if you will, he was at the Union Centre when it happened.

There were many who thought the world was ending because the U.S. had invaded Iraq. When it comes to taking political action, I think the idea of imminent threat is what makes the difference for some. Most demonstrations in Winnipeg are doing great with more than 150 people in attendance. That number is just about the average for a demonstration, no matter what the cause. The peace groups have their community, labour has their community and you bring them together and this is what you get: two hundred people, with speeches and some noise. Why do so few people participate in demonstrations? There are so many factors at play: television, which keeps people inside, political indifference and even the lack of desire for community in general. But Winnipeg's history is peppered with large-scale political activity, the kind of citizenship that I love to see. The General Strike of 1919 had masses of people out to huge rallies and demonstrations. That was when the communists and others armed with baseball bats beat the shit out of the South End crowd. I read through Roland Penner's biography where he talks about May Day in 1935 when he was only eleven years old and I remember Winnipeg's strong history of demonstrating.

I've been to some demonstrations with tense moments. In June 2004, Peace Alliance Winnipeg asked me to be chief marshal of a demonstration. Darrell Rankin, leader of the Manitoba Communist Party and one of the peace demonstration organizers, was not able to get a permit to march on the street because there was a farewell parade of the Second Battalion, Princess Patricia's Canadian Light Infantry, scheduled for the same day. I wasn't aware of this fact when I agreed to marshal. Here we were, marching on the streets, when the cops came; there was a good crowd of people but I had the bullhorn. The officers asked me to move the march to the sidewalk while participants marched eastbound on Broadway Avenue. I gave the marchers the option of moving to the sidewalk or staying on the roadway illegally and the crowd decided to stay on the road. Next, someone started a chant, "Stay on the street!" which the police responded to by surrounding me and handcuffing me. I was the leader, shouting the slogans, and so I was the target. They had no business doing this because they didn't charge me with anything. After they put me in the patrol car, the demonstration stopped and the crowd surrounded the car. There must have been two hundred protesters, maybe more, and they were angry. The cops got on their phones and must have been told to let me go as things could have become bad in a hurry.

They let us finish the march on the road without incident but three days later they came to my house and charged me with infractions of the *Highway Traffic Act*: staging a march without a permit, jaywalking and ignoring a police officer's instructions. The charge made headlines and we took it to court. A three thousand dollar fine was possible.

I received an absolute discharge for disobeying a police officer and had the permit violation charges dropped. It was accepted that I had indicated to the police officers who the organisers were, and it was accepted that the police chose to ignore that information and press charges on me. I passed on the information to the crowd, just like the officers asked me to. The crowd disobeyed, but not me.

In court, I had my chance to make a speech to the judge. I argued that they asked me to be an agent of the police. My lawyer, Ian Histed, cited my ongoing battle with cancer and contributions to the community as grounds for leniency. He criticized police for pulling me out of a crowd of 250 people. He said I was "singled out because of my celebrity status." Earlier that year, anti-mosquito fogging demonstrator Glenda Whiteman received an absolute discharge on similar charges. Judge Howard Collerman called her actions "courageous." I received no such praise. The judge gave no punishment, no fine, no nothing. He said, "I am dismissing this," even though he had to find me guilty as charged with jaywalking. The cops were furious! As I keep saying, I've beaten the police every time I've had any dealings with them. In fact, I would have welcomed charges, as it would have given us a chance to make a constitutional challenge to the police chief's right to dispense parade permits arbitrarily, without any accountability. The "No War Coalition" was even collecting money for my defence fund for the jaywalking charges but there ended up being nothing to defend. Within a year, a new by-law law was written to clarify the limits and give the police chief direction in responding to parade permit applications.

This sign of collective inaction — the dwindling numbers at marches and demonstrations — is accompanied by another: the ever-decreasing level of voting. I have tried to talk to younger people and others who don't vote, and I wrote incessantly on that issue with my *Left Punch* columns in the Winnipeg weekly *Uptown*. What comes back to me is their understanding that it doesn't matter who you elect, nothing will change. I see this as an intentional declaration: "I will not vote because by voting I will confirm the

Nick speaking for peace in the Middle East

hypocrisy of the political system as I know it." It is not my response, but I understand where it comes from. They do not want to legitimize a system they see as corrupt. Blaming youth for being lazy is too easy, is inaccurate and avoids the issues that have produced their apathy.

Through my ongoing connection with Peace Alliance Winnipeg, I participated in annual events such as Hiroshima Day (as an alternative to Remembrance Day) and the annual Peace Walk in June. In addition, other events came up and got me out, such as the protest over the military focus of the air show (while Winnipeg still had one). Then there was our NDP Premier Gary Doer promoting a yellow ribbon "support our troops campaign," feeling no need to reconcile that position with the NDP's fundamental opposition to war.

There has been no period in human history where the voice for peace was not needed; this is certainly true in my life — the peace movement never ends. The struggle for an end to war is ongoing, and I have never left it since 1968 when I was approached to organize a single rally. I have done a lot of marching for peace, supporting ongoing reactions to developments in Palestine, Yugolslavia, Afghanistan and other such international and military conflicts. It is a matter of committing to the idea that if you are not part of the solution, you are part of the problem. Suspicion and fear are at the root of violence. The peace movement's work is to offset the forces in our society that promote suspicion and fear.

5

The Scene in the
Sixties and Seventies

"When awareness is triggered, people can then have the kind of life-changing experience that engages them in the process of their own change and revolution. Ask what makes me tick, and that is my answer: I am part of that larger revolution."

I will never lose sight of the fact that I am a product of the sixties. I was as active in the counterculture as I was in the political movement. Few straddled those boundaries. The left had their own political perspectives and did their own activities. In a word, they were sectarian. Some even had their own bookstores. There were quite a variety of groups on the left in Winnipeg at the time. There was the Communist Party of Canada (CPC), of course, and CPC (Marxist-Leninist), who were very much into the thinking of Mao Tse-Tung (seeing leftist revolution as being led by a small group of committed people). Trotskyist groups — those who also believed in a vanguard revolutionary group, but thought that socialism could be achieved in non-industrial countries — included the League of Socialist Action (LSA) and their youth group, the Young Socialists, the Revolutionary Marxist Group (RMG) and, after the LSA and RMG fused, the Revolutionary Workers League (RWL). There were also independent socialists, some of whom organized around the magazine *Canadian Dimension*, the Waffle group at the left end of the New Democratic Party and, then, the rest of the NDP. Most of these groups were quite small, mind you, and it's worth mentioning that, in the sixties and seventies, most of the people who identified as left were active in the NDP.

The Co-op Bookstore was for the communists. Roland Penner was one of its founders back in the fifties. He gives some history of the bookstore in his memoir, *A Glowing Dream*. He tells stories from its beginning on Main Street to where it ended on Donald Street near Notre Dame Avenue, which is actually only a few blocks away from where the Mondragon Bookstore and Coffeehouse now operates as a co-op. From 1963 to 1971 Floyd Williston ran the store. Then Nancy Watkins ran it until 1994; by the end it sold clothes with progressive slogans as well as books. Up until the collapse of the Soviet Union, the bookstore was subsidized by the Communist Party; the loss of that money contributed to the bookstore's closure after forty-one years of business.

Floyd really opened it up and carried books for the Trotskyites, the Maoists, the Marxists and just about any left-progressive group that would buy books. It became a real gathering place in the late sixties for all kinds of people, from the premier all the way to the most obtuse radical. There was music going on there too. Mitch Podolak, who went on to be the founder of the Winnipeg Folk Festival, was one of the people who was around a lot, and he and Floyd both did some great things, like bringing Pete Seeger in to Playhouse Theatre in 1969. José Feliciano played at a small dinner cafe on Donald called The Establishment. Floyd tells a story of asking Feliciano if he suffered prejudice from being blind and how he answered: "No one discriminates against José Feliciano."

The Trotskyites had a bookstore that lasted about a year and the Monkey Tree, run by Jim McGregor, was a commercial bookstore that had a Maoist section. It was at Portage Avenue and Edmonton Street, where the Portage Place mall is now. Jim was never able to reopen the store after a fire above it caused major water damage. I worked at both the bookstores in sales. At the Monkey Tree, they had me reaching out to sell the four essays by Mao Tse Tung. At the Co-op Bookstore, I worked with Floyd Williston in 1966 and if I walked in late he would announce, "Here comes Nick Ternette, late for the revolution. The revolution started at 10 a.m. Nick missed it!" He'll still joke about that when he sees me.

These were more than bookstores. They were meeting places where like-minded people could come together. Both formal lectures and much less formal discussion sessions helped people both understand and dream about the revolution. Every city had these places springing up or coming into a new life.

The bookstores were related to another pillar of change in the late sixties and early seventies: education. One of my good friends is Lawrie Cherniack, whose father was Saul Cherniack, Minister of Finance in the

Schreyer NDP government. Lawrie became a labour lawyer, but when I first met him in 1968, he had just come from the University of Chicago, where he had graduated with a master's degree in literature. Like others, he wanted to become the greatest novelist of his time and he still tells me that he wants to be a novelist. Although various people were involved, he was the true founding force of the Free University in Winnipeg in 1968. We connected when I phoned the number on a poster he had put up to recruit teachers. He will still tell the story about how his arms weren't long enough to talk with me on the phone. He said that I talked so loud that even when he held the phone at arm's length, my voice was so loud it sounded like I was yelling. He taught a course on author Herman Melville, and had only five people in his class. I had thirty to forty people coming to my class on revolution so he may have been a bit jealous of my numbers, but that didn't make him any less passionate about what he was teaching. Later, he became a community organizer for the Institute of Urban Studies and worked for Lloyd Axworthy while he was running it. From there he won a seat on city council in 1971 before going back to school to study law. His father had suggested that unless he had a profession to fall back on he could be in danger of compromising his principles to ensure he would be elected and have a job. He became a great lawyer and made a good living. That's what happens to people. He is still a very progressive person, but you settle down and you have a career. It works that way.

The Free University started out, in the summer of 1968, at the YMCA, and within a few months moved to what is now St. Matthew's Maryland Church, with more than forty courses offered. The first eight courses offered were varied and included topics such as Sex Hygiene, Moral Philosophy and Practical Mysticism. Success followed with a move to a house in Osborne Village but the energy and coordination fizzled after moving to a similar venue on Main Street. While it lasted there were some great courses and it stayed true to its roots of "free learning" and a "forum rather than a training ground," as described in its promotional literature. I liked to use guests in my course on civic politics. Maurice Gauthier, a great leader in the Franco-Manitoban Community, came and spoke about the co-op movement. My friend Norm Larsen came and spoke about legal aid. Lawyer Jack Bass, with whom I would later host a television program, spoke on the role of contracts in civil discourse. The Free University was part of a much larger movement.

Even Liberal politicians like Bobby Bend, who would become the provincial leader, knew that our education system didn't promote open thinking. The Free University was committed to avoiding structure and to building a community of free thought. We all felt that existing universities were overly structured and prevented true community and freethinking.

Free universities were all over the world, including well-known schools in Berlin and Amsterdam and, of course, Rochdale College in Toronto, Canada's most successful

The 1960s radical

experiment of its kind. Rochdale was much more extensive than Winnipeg's free school, with a large residence and a commitment to freedom in all things. I kept the application I got from them. Among the many treasures were rooms named after Kafka and the promise that "living in the typical Rochdalian intensity helps you discover what the entity using your name and body is really like." You will find an incredible number of people my age who will say they lived there. It is quite possible, as some estimates say, that the "crashers" outnumbered the actual rent payers by a ratio of ten to one. I was one of the "crashers." I stayed there for two weeks when I went to Toronto to meet up with my friend Dmitri Roussopoulos. The *Globe & Mail* was doing some story on the place and somehow I happened to get in the picture they printed of a small meeting I attended. Plentiful are the people who have stories to tell about their time in Rochdale; more plentiful may be those who can't remember their stories. It was an incredible hotbed of drug use, and while there were lofty goals and commitments, not much was realized.

Eventually, the University of Manitoba took over the Free University and I continued to teach at it. It finally ended in the late seventies and by then it had lost a lot of its power and its implicit critique of the education system. The days of the real independent free school movement from 1968 to 1971, when I taught the course in revolution, were the best. It was a true vanguard! Later on, the domesticated version out of the University of Manitoba, where I taught courses in civic affairs and urban politics, were still enjoyable and varied but not as invigorating for me. Macrobiotics, Electronics, Basic Law, Geology and Decision Making in Relationships were all part of the course offerings.

Another response to the inadequate and limited education system was the Festival of Life and Learning. It began a year after the Free University ran a one-time "Festival of Life and Learning." In the early seventies, university students wanted to create an environment for intellectual challenge including theatre and music, and in the early days the Festival was quite radical. From 1970 to 1975, the Festival promoted all kinds of radical forums that opened up new ways of thinking and living. That edge just became dulled with time, and a few years ago the event was subsumed into "Celebration Week" and any ties with its radical past were put to rest forever. In its early days, the Festival of Life and Learning was held both at the University of Winnipeg and University of Manitoba and its purpose was to offer fundamentally different visions of art and culture, mixing the university with the community in a unique and challenging way. They were taking new risks, reaching out to the community and not staying in the proverbial ivory tower. We had a speakers' corner right downtown with people speaking to whoever would listen. I gave a speech about civil liberties and my arrest for demonstrating at the Festival Express concert.

The left flatly rejected all sorts of great initiatives of the day because they were seen as something less than a revolution. Klinic, for example, was established as the counter institution in order to deal with drug addiction and other social problems that impacted people's health. They are still doing great things in West Broadway and the West End of Winnipeg. CRYPT, the Community Representing Youth Problems of Today, was a liberal organization of social workers and others who were concerned about the kids who travelled all over the place and didn't have a place to stay. Most of them stayed at Memorial Park, but in the winter the streets and parks of Winnipeg lack hospitality. On an average night two to three hundred people might be found sleeping at the park. It was a bit of a mixed crowd with bikers, hippies and other people who thought it was the best place to sleep. I would have people sleeping on the floor in my apartment for a dollar a night and this connected me with CRYPT. I wound up helping them have a demonstration, which had no connection with the left in terms of demanding shelter. We had similar events to demand the creation of new social agencies to meet the emerging needs of these young people creating their own culture.

CRYPT ran out of funding, and the province, under the leadership of Cabinet Minister Rene Toupin, eventually took over their work. The take-over was hostile. They just announced they would assume administrative and policy control and they undermined the entire energy that brought us success. Power, in this case, bred fear. With these developments, Ron Wally, their director, left CRYPT and became director of Non-Medical Use of Drugs, a federal agency. CRYPT was decimated by government control, and Peace in this House (PITH) replaced it. Klinic, first thought about and discussed by the CRYPT group, developed from the energy of Ron Wally, Bruce McManus and others. It was initially run out of the Health Sciences Centre as a place for transient youth coping with drug overdoses; now it is an extremely comprehensive community centre for health treatment, advocacy and education. The groundwork came from 1968 within CRYPT and the establishment of the lasting institutions came after incorporation in 1973.

By the end of 1972, the countercultural movement was all but dead. Klinic is one of the few institutions still remaining from those days, with the others being the Main Street Project and Community Income Tax Service (CITS). Aside from these few, the rest — including all sorts of hostels and drop-in centres — just faded and faded quickly.

In 1971, Greg Selinger, our current premier, had just graduated from the School of Social Work at the University of Manitoba, and his first job was in community development. One of his concerns was overcharging for filling out tax returns. He and I and a few others publically called these charges usury fees. Private sector tax return services were charging as much as ninety percent of people's refunds. We formed a free income tax service — Community Income Tax Service — using government money. Manitoba Premier Schreyer was open to that sort of thing at the time. Then, the credit union movement got involved and we decided to establish a credit union in the core area and opened the Midland Credit Union on Isabel Street. Eventually it shut down, likely because they were charging such low rates of interest and having too many loans that defaulted. We calculated later that what people paid about $6000 for would have cost over $200,000 had the private tax services done the work. Our service would advance tax money at one percent interest. This knocked the Calgary-based loan sharks out of business and we redistributed millions of dollars back into the core area. In 1975, I went to Ottawa and negotiated with Tom Axworthy, Assistant to the Minister of Finance in the Liberal Government, to try to get legislation to limit the interest these companies could charge. It took two years to get the legislation, but we did. Victories seemed to come few and far between in my life, so I tend to remember them. This one was big. Colin Muir and, even more so, Greg Selinger, were the brains and the brawn behind this. I was just around to see it. It is rather ironic that, with all his hard work and success back then, Selinger, first as finance minister and then as premier, has all sorts of payday loans outfits and income tax filing services doing the very same thing we shut down forty years ago. I know he cares about these issues, as does anyone who knows the way these places operate and who is affected by what they do. Selinger has since passed some legislation limiting the interest that can be charged by payday loan companies.

Although the original organization is long gone, we were able to transfer a million and half dollars of assets when the credit union closed. The name for the rest of the organization was changed to Community Financial Counselling Services (CFCS) to reflect that fact they mostly do debt counselling these days while other groups have picked up free income tax preparations. Community organizations recruit volunteers to complete and submit tax claims electronically, meaning that rebates come back in a matter of weeks if not days and users do not incur exorbitant charges for the services. If you are in debt and you're poor, CFCS will negotiate with the banks and financial institutions so you don't have to go into bankruptcy. They are a very good organization. Community organizing was never a priority of the left in Winnipeg. There were natural links between leftist groups and grassroots community initiatives — the core group of people was small and everyone knew each other — but a cohesive effort just did not happen. There were exceptions — the communists built a network of co-ops in the North End, the People's Co-op creamery being one of the most important and long lasting, and Joe Zuken was deeply rooted in the North End community, for example — but generally the left groups focused on national and international efforts, and ideology. Most of the Trotskyites and the Maoists spent their time on university campuses. I am not saying that opposing the Vietnam War wasn't important, but that is where they put all their energy.

This is one of the reasons I admire Jim Silver so much. He is a professor at the University of Winnipeg who makes these very connections every day and, more importantly, he has access to students to help them do the same. I met Jim when he came to Calgary, early in my time there, with his partner Loa Henry, who was the director of the Nellie McClung Theatre group, which was on tour. He had come from Ontario and he was not around Winnipeg in the seventies. I came to work with him and had the opportunity to get to know him much better after I moved back to Winnipeg in 1986.

From 1969 to 1973, I lived in an apartment on Fort Street where I housed "The People's Cooperative." This was my first move out of my parents' house. It wasn't ever a co-op in the sense of having a true business model, but it was a place where those interested in leftist ideas could gather and talk. Because I got along with people so well, everyone felt comfortable being there and we had local musicians playing there too. It was a lot more than just a place to live. This is also where I had as many as dozen transient youth sleeping on the floor. I was the caretaker of that building and dealt only with the management company but found out later that it was one of the buildings owned by long-time Manitoba Conservative Party politician Sidney Spivak. It was torn down when the Trizac Building was built.

The co-operative never really took off the way I had hoped but a lot happened in that apartment. I used to charge a dollar a night for homeless transients who were trying to make their way from Eastern Canada to Vancouver. Yes, I had a house full of hippies almost every night, every summer. That apartment was also the site of the very first meetings of Winnipeg feminists, who had lost their original meeting space. Once a week or so, I would have to leave when they had their meeting. Lissa Donner, Evelyn Ste. Croix, lin gibson, Pat Stainton, Helen Nelson and others would come to my apartment to meet and plan actions around abortion rights and other matters germane to the budding women's movement. Some of this history is in the report written for the CCPA–Manitoba, *In for the Long Haul: Women's Organizations in Manitoba*, written by Joan Grace. It is a quiet privilege to have been a small part of such important beginnings.

While the idea of the Neighbourhood Services Centres (NSC) dates back to the 1890s, in the late sixties and early seventies the community development experiment in Winnipeg went to a new level. The NSC came out of Logan House, a neighbourhood social service agency located just off Logan Street (on 294 Ellen Street), providing recreation for kids and things like that. It became NSC when it decided, independently but part of a continent-wide shift in social work thinking, to change from a service-providing, neighbourhood-based agency to more of a community-organizing agency. With several layers of funding, including a little money from the Schreyer NDP government but mostly from charity foundations such as the United Way, workers at the centres were given a wide mandate for assisting in poor neighbourhoods.

My work with the NSC, which was a paid position, lasted three and a half years and gave me opportunities to connect with all sorts of initiatives at their beginning. For example, I helped fund Community Income Tax Service (CITS) in 1971 through NSC. As well, I was connected to a food buyer's club, which was a food-purchasing co-op that essentially predated the food banks in the city. I also was around when an early journalist's co-op tried to form Winnipeg's first community radio station. All ideas were worth considering and projects sprung up all the time. If they didn't stay around, it wasn't an issue — something else would come around.

The NSC was fundamentally involved in the life of the city — "little city halls" — that connected people from all different places. There were five staff people. Tim Maloney was exceedingly bright. He later became an area director for the Children's Aid Society in Manitoba and held leadership positions in that field across Canada. He remains an activist in many areas and has recently been involved in seeking to welcome war resisters from the United States into Canada. Tim and I were the two most comfortable with being "out there," causing trouble. Bernie Nelson was a damn good organizer and Sharon Stelmachuk also worked for us for a while. This was an incredible collection of youthful talent. Arni Arnason was executive director and the way we lived out his vision really set us free! We could work anywhere in Winnipeg, wherever groups of people wanted to get together and were concerned about issues. We could work with those groups and organize them to make improvements. It was incredibly visionary and highly motivating to use resources the way we did.

I worked sixty to seventy hours a week and was out at meetings every night but never worried because it was exactly what I wanted to be doing.

I worked with Olga Foltz in a welfare rights organization. She was the one also who started the self-help divorce organization with Joe Zuken. Olga and I got along well in this work but, much later, in 1986, we had disagreements when I was supposed to be doing a practicum for my social work degree and she didn't want me at the NSC. I ended up working with Doug Martindale at Stella Mission on housing and other income-related issues.

In 1974, I helped Olga strategize on a how to get a petition on a guaranteed annual income to then premier Ed Schreyer. He lived off Henderson Highway, and I knew that, because of his Ukrainian-German background, he would be home on Christmas Eve, so we packed this petition into a beautiful gift box and wrapped it up. Arni Arnason, my boss, drove me out there at two o'clock in the afternoon. I figured Schreyer would just take the gift and say thank you and goodbye to us. Schreyer and I had been on opposite sides in battles at NDP conventions so I was shocked, frankly, when he invited us in.

Next thing you know he brings out Heineken beer and he starts talking about everything under the sun. For two and a half hours, I'm sitting drinking his beer and listening to his stories. He had taken the gift and put it under the Christmas tree. I should have known he would do that because he wasn't a suspicious man. His wife, Lil, looked at me as if she didn't know why the hell I had shown up with a gift on Christmas Eve, but she didn't really have a chance to say much being busy with other things. Even before I left, I was feeling a little embarrassed at how nice he was treating me when we were really up to something to embarrass him. Later I learned that when they opened their presents later that night, on Christmas Eve, he opened the box in front of his family and some friends and was not mad at all. I was told that he smiled, and looked at the petition and actually read it. Lil, on the other hand, wouldn't talk to me for over a year. I think I did Saul Alinsky proud that day.

In fact, all of us at the NSC, to varying degrees, had been introduced to the teachings of Saul Alinsky and were keen to get into action even if not following Alinsky's prescriptions. I met Saul Alinsky when I attended a national conference as a representative of the University of Winnipeg that included the Company of Young Canadians and some other radical youth in New Brunswick in 1966 and again in 1970 when he came to Winnipeg to speak at the Festival of Life and Learning. He ripped into me when I asked a question about the new left in front of four hundred people, but was kind and attentive over the next few days of his visit when we visited social agencies and the like together. In New Brunswick and other places, he tore social workers to shreds, talking about entirely new ways of building and being community and not just being a band-aid that was part of the system of oppression. He just sat on stage chain smoking and talking. His ideas were brilliant.

I read what Alinksy I could after finishing university in 1970 and found a series of films by the National Film Board of Canada that captured his spirit very well. One was a debate between him and a young native leader, Duke Redbird. Alinsky's teachings were stark and on the edge. They demanded a reaction. Everybody has used his book, *Rules for Radicals*. Even the Republican Party in the U.S. has used it. He became a centre stage radical in unprecedented ways. This culminated in a feature interview he did with *Playboy* magazine. Alinsky was the organizer of organizers. Giving the premier a petition for Christmas was right out of his playbook. In *Rules for Radicals*, he states the purpose of his writing: "so the Have Nots [know] how to take [power] away [from those who hold it]." That pretty much sums up what I have tried to do as well.

The NSC also worked in Brooklands — a North End neighbourhood south of Logan Avenue. Bernie Nelson was very diligent and focused in this area. I just supported where I could. We helped the residents there whose homes were set for expropriation. We helped start some of the first tenants' organizations in Winnipeg, raising the profile of the slum housing in the city. Tim Maloney had an especially high profile. He had come to Canada because of the draft, having fled the United States during the Vietnam War. The labels "radical" and "activist" were not ones we used on ourselves. The media used those words and others picked them up. We were just doing what we thought should be done. Eventually, once we heard them enough, we started to think of ourselves in those terms, and I still do. The media liked us and eventually they were taking their leads from us on a regular basis. They were either lazy or smart, or both. They knew I was aware of what was going on so they were in touch with me all the time, and I with them.

There was tension at the NSC throughout this exciting time because the United Way, the principal funder, was uncomfortable with our political stands. Eventually I left the NSC because it was clear we would have to either move in a different direction or lose our core funding. Even though Maloney and I left, it was less than a year before the United Way pulled the funding and the work we were doing came to an end.

The sixties and seventies also brought liberal use of drugs like marijuana and LSD, and sexual freedom. My interests were more in the political realm and that actually made some people wonder if I was a police agent or a spy of some kind. Eventually I grew a big beard and let my hair get long and I looked more the part, but I never used the word "hippie" to describe myself, even though they surrounded me all the time. The hippies were middle and upper class; that is why they saw not working as an option. If they ran out of money, they phoned Mommy.

I was in favour, as were many, of legalizing cannabis. In fact, there was a Winnipeg event held in the early seventies where Donald Benham, who was active with the Young Conservatives, and I both caught shit from our parties for speaking in favour of legalizing pot. That is where and how Donald and I met and we have been friends ever since. I have always been in favour of legalizing marijuana in order to garner income from taxing it, rather than using precious resources to police it.

The whole movement for social justice change began caving early in the seventies. Many people just "aged out" and wanted to get on with their careers. Others ended up being hooked on harder drugs or paid the price of the lifestyle with sexually transmitted diseases. Mostly, though, the social justice movement was a middle-class phenomenon and, after being distracted for a few years, its participants got back on the middle-class program. These are the people hitting retirement age right now; for many, the sixties were just a small blip, many, many years ago, and many of them don't want known exactly what went on. Others kept some of their ideals and became Liberals or centrist NDPers, but most moved on from the radical openness that those years created. I chose then to never be part of the establishment and aside from a few odd moments where I have been honoured as "an exemplary citizen," I have been anything but the establishment.

I had some overlap with the hippie movement because, like them, I was anti-materialist. Even though many of them had the safety net of their rich families, they were living away from it as they lived out the hippie lifestyle. Travel was the other overlap. Getting around was cheap in those days, and perhaps we were all a little inspired by Kerouac's *On the Road*. It was nothing for me to get in a car with a bunch of other people and drive halfway across the country for a conference in the Maritimes, Quebec or Ontario. Gas was cheap. The environmental costs of driving across the country just to go to a concert or hear a speaker were nowhere on the horizon. I never had my driver's licence. My father had taken me driving once and I crashed into a tree so I took the hint and never got behind the wheel again. Fortunately, there were always people happy to drive. I met so many people travelling. I was a minor figure for sure, but I spent time with the authentic voices and thinkers of the left. I got to know the people at *Our Generation*, a Montreal-based journal of libertarian socialism with an anarchist bent. Dmitri Roussopoulos was one of the leaders of the anarchist movement of Canada and I got to know him. In those travels I also met my personal heroes, Saul Alinsky and musician Phil Ochs.

The sixties and seventies in Winnipeg were also marked by publishing starts. *Omphalos* was an underground newspaper that was the brainchild of English professor Arthur Adamson. Leonard Anderson, Kelly Clark and Cy Gonick were some of the other people who were involved in starting it. This paper was uniquely successful in bringing the political and social circles together where they would cross the each other's boundaries. There is an entire chapter devoted to an extensive history of *Omphalos* in Ron Verzuh's book *Underground Times*. Among other things he talks about where the name "Omphalos" came from: Adamson knew it from a James Joyce work and Anderson liked it because it means navel, and was seen by the Greeks to be the seat of the soul. Arthur Adamson passed away under tragic circumstances many years ago but I remain friends with his cousin, Shirley Kowalchuck, and we remember him whenever we meet.

I worked directly with Cy Gonick a number of times. Cy started *Canadian Dimension* in Saskatchewan but moved it to Winnipeg almost immediately when he got a post at the University of Manitoba in the 1960s. 2012 marks the fiftieth year of *Canadian Dimension*. I also worked with Cy in the Winnipeg Unemployed Committee. He organized it and I ended up being the secretary. We got some good press; this was back in 1971, when, comparatively, unemployment was not a big issue. I attended the Poor People's Congress in Ottawa in 1969, because I listed my apartment on Fort Street as a co-op and they invited all the co-ops in the country. I went with the head of the Council of Self-Help, Durlene Germsheid, and a few others. One of the proposals was to organize poor people's parliaments in each of our own cities. Ray Torgrud had me on CKY-TV to talk about this idea, which I believe was my first television experience. We booked city hall for people's parliament to happen for a whole day in January 1971 and had two follow-up sessions. It all came together very quickly after our original meeting. The head of the Welfare Appeal Board, Una Decter, was in charge. George McLeod and Gerald Kinney were also in leadership and I was one of the delegates. Wally Denison, who retired to British Columbia, was a reporter who cared about social matters and he provided some great coverage. It is just hard to imagine the political will to do such things today.

We brought a truly holistic approach to our work with the poor people's parliament and covered very broad topics, asking such questions as "Where is the wealth?" "How do we support the disabled?" "How do we address Aboriginal rights?" "the Quebec issue?" "Black issues?" and others. Some great suggestions were put forth and, looking back forty-plus years later, it can be quite alarming to see how little has changed or been accomplished. Out of the nine recommendations put forth for prison issues, for example, none are present in our provincial system. Prisoners still leave the jail broke. Segregation is still used on a far too regular basis. Remand and sentenced inmates are still mingled in such a way that programming and rehabilitation efforts are impeded. Ex-convicts have a wealth of information to share on prison reform but they are not consulted in any meaningful way. Staff training is still woefully inadequate to work with the complexity of problems that inmates bring forward.

Another group I worked with was the Council of Self-Help. I was an advisor on welfare and related issues. They did not have an executive director and in fact seemed to be on their last legs without any staff, so they interviewed and hired me. Durlene Germsheid had been there and left to work at the Human Rights Commission. There had been a year with another director but this experience is kind of a metaphor for my life. I walked onto a sinking ship while everybody else was clambering to get off. The United Way had funded the Council in the early seventies as part of their anti-poverty initiatives and, given the context, it quickly became militant and radical. Organizational structure was far down the list of priorities. Welfare, at that time, was shared by the province and city so I spent a lot of time at city hall, advocating and talking to the press about the injustices in the system.

I remember the School of Social Work working on a book called *Know Your Welfare Rights* and they had hired three students to do the research. Derek Shettler, Jennifer Wells and Bill Millar actually did the work but I took the public hit for it and it should have been that way. With the semi-implosion of the Council for Self-Help, I ended up inheriting the task of finishing the book. We managed to get it printed but it was immediately controversial because it pointed out the hypocrisy of bureaucrats and talked about how bureaucrats dealt with people. It had sketches of how to apply for welfare and listed the things to look out for and the right way to answer the questions in order to get benefits. We attacked the status quo and that was very threatening to many. They wanted us just to hold people's hands and have them put up with the system. Ron Hooper, the city welfare director, claimed the handbook fostered a negative image of welfare that would lead to an adverse effect on his staff's relationship with recipients. He pointed to our introduction that read, "This is written for people in a welfare system that desperately needs improvement." This is the way of the right wing: anything that questions the way things are is considered negative. Calling something negative is then grounds for dismissal. Truth has no value. We ended up having to demand an apology from him when he banned the publication from welfare offices and called us liars. In fact, the students had been very diligent with their fact checking and had used Norm Larson from the Community Law Office for the technical legal points. The students called themselves Linc, Julie and Pete after the three characters on the Mod Squad TV show. Derrick had the curliest hair so he got to be Linc, who sported an afro. They were also affected, and to some extent, radicalized by the process — seeing how welfare assistance purported to be a solution but, in fact, was often part of the problem. It is a project I am thankful to have been connected with even though I could hardly say that people on welfare these days know and demand what is rightfully their due.

Poverty was a crucial issue in the early seventies and there was a movement for a national day of protest. Una Decter put forth the idea of holding a "Poverty Day" at city hall, where the poor people would take over city hall and would bring up issues related to poverty and welfare. I had to negotiate to get city hall for one day, but in fact Una took the lead. Her diplomatic skills were far beyond mine. We were able to pull this off, even though the energy to continue with Poverty Day slipped over the years.

We had all these welfare organizations and social agencies doing this; there was a feature story in the *Winnipeg Free Press* by Wally Dennison and it really raised awareness.

Doing a thing like Poverty Day is what activism is: raising awareness. When awareness is triggered, people can then have the kind of life-changing experience that engages them in the process of their own change and revolution. Ask what makes me tick, and that is my answer: I am part of that larger revolution.

Part of the vision of the time was a realization that we all had much to learn from each other and this gave me the opportunity to travel quite a bit to symposiums and conferences. One that was particularly energizing was a gathering of six hundred community development workers in Colorado. We heard about government-funded, community-based, citizen-initiated projects delivering their own services and what a big change that was making. It was this thought that drove what we were doing. It was anything but "dropping out." It was about "jumping in" to society and engaging with the very problems you lived with.

You can't think of the sixties and seventies in Winnipeg without thinking of the music. My mother was an artist — I still have her paintings on my walls — and my father was into classical music. I was raised with the idea that art and music were part of the fabric of life. My father liked classical tenors. He listened to Russians like Boris Shtokolov but also liked Mario Lanza. He listened to the opera every Saturday on CBC Radio and I would sit and listen with him. I doubt that many teenagers of my time were doing this. I didn't really embrace it; it just came with the house I lived in. Because of this, though, I didn't really follow a lot of the music in the sixties. I gravitated much more to folk than rock. We had coffee houses; we called them "hootenannies," where there was an open stage for folk singers. It was popular not only at Winnipeg's United College but across the continent.

As the folk scene was also starting to come around, there were two places in Winnipeg that stood out. The Fourth Dimension, which was a coffee shop, was dark and smoky. They painted everything completely black. To me, it was just ugly. It was on Pembina Highway, by the entrance to the University of Manitoba, but the "4-D," as we called it, was the place to be in the sixties. Buffy Saint-Marie, Joni Mitchell, Neil Young and others all played there.

The other place was The Ting at 595 Broadway, which since has been a variety of restaurants and now houses a sexual health outreach program. The Ting was a tearoom where people would meet. It was small, with booths, but roomy for a good crowd. I would meet there with people like Ron Wally, the head of CRYPT, who went on to be a labour leader, and Tim Maloney, who was head of the draft dodgers' group. This is where people met and talked. They had fantastic musicians at The Ting too. I will never forget seeing Lenny Breau play his ten-string guitar there.

These were the two places where the sixties folk scene happened in Winnipeg. One of the folk singers I met in 1966 was a local guy named Fred Penner. He sang the folk songs of the day and he had a few of his own. He was a protest singer when he started and now there are at least two if not three generations in Canada and beyond who know him as a kid's entertainer and TV personality. I have stayed friends with Fred ever since. In January of 2012, he sang at my birthday and played some of those great old protest songs out of his copy of *Rise Up Singing* as well as a tribute song he wrote for me on a napkin at the party. He also did his two classics, "Sandwiches" and "The Cat Came Back," much to the delight of all my friends who had joined me at the Ellice Café.

In 1967, the Mitchell Trio played in Winnipeg and I didn't have a clue who they were. We knew it was a hootenanny and we knew that Floyd Williston had brought them in. They were fantastic. One of the members was John Denver. Most people don't think of John Denver as a performer of critical political folk music in the 1960s. Most of us think about his soft country hits, and he even performed "Leaving on a Jet Plane" that night. It must have been one of the first times. Peter, Paul and Mary, who had the bigger hit with it, didn't record it until 1969. I love memories like that concert. They remind me where I came from.

I also saw Simon and Garfunkel play in the old Winnipeg Auditorium, which was our concert hall before we built the new one in our centennial year. That building is now our provincial archives on Vaughn Street. When they saw all the hippies who were in Memorial Park, Simon and Garfunkel went over and just hung out with them. It is a great moment in Winnipeg music history. It is up there with Janis Joplin jumping in the fountain at Memorial Park when she arrived in Winnipeg on the Musical Express tour. These places and that music were the backdrop of my emergence as a left-wing activist.

I think most of us have a "soundtrack" to our life. My favourite folk singer is still Phil Ochs. It is amazing how few people have even heard of him. He was probably the most political performer there ever was. When he committed suicide in 1976, I really wanted to get to a special concert held in his honour in New York in the Felt Forum, a theatre in Madison Square Garden. I wasn't able to but I made my own tribute by writing a biographical script and interspersing it with cuts of music on air on CJUM, the University of Manitoba's radio station at the time. He really had been an inspiration for me so I had to do something in response to his tragic death.

I had met him at Glendon College in Toronto after I had seen him in a concert during the Year of the Barricades Conference. He was keen to come to Winnipeg, and his rate, $2,000, was quite reasonable. I thought the University of Manitoba would bring him but they balked at the price, so he never did play Winnipeg. His song "Love me, Love me, I'm a Liberal" is my favourite of all songs and is as relevant today as the day he wrote it.

The times really were different. They really were a changin'! The cries of the music supported the shouts of the political and vice versa. A few years ago at the Winnipeg Folk Festival there were all sorts of protests after a folk singer, Geoff Berner, sang a song called "Maginot Line" and introduced it by reminding the audience of Volkswagen's association with Adolf Hitler. He explained how during the 1930s, production of the "people's car" was promoted as a means of dealing with unemployment during the Nazi period. Can you imagine Mitch Podolak, founder of the Folk Festival and a Jewish Trotskyist, apologizing to Volkswagen, now a sponsor of the festival, because of a protest song sung from the stage? The sixties were a time of great permission to explore and a great time to be in your twenties. We didn't worry about crap like keeping "our sponsors" happy.

Bill Landin, George McLeod and Kasmir Panuta and I lived together from 1972 to 1979. We were in an apartment for a year and then in a house at 153 Lenore for six years when the sale of the house ended the arrangement. Rent was seventy-five dollars each, a great deal. A number of people came and left as well but that was the core. George founded the Cooperative Employment Agency, which facilitated temporary jobs on a not-for-profit basis. He was a little older than the rest of us, and he is the one who put his name on the lease. Bill was with the Company of Young Canadians and later moved to British Columbia before coming back to Manitoba, where he eventually became mayor of Cartwright, in southwestern Manitoba. Kasmir, whom I had met a CRYPT, worked at the St. Amant Centre for a long time and eventually became a teacher in St. Vital before his retirement. It was a good economic set-up: we had meals together sometimes but it wasn't like we were selling ourselves as an alternative community or a commune. It was affordable cooperative living.

My daughter Tegan was born when I lived there. I have to admit I have never really been comfortable with women. I was raised by a very dominant mother in a loveless marriage. I was brought up in the Russian Orthodox Church, which taught that the only purpose of sex was for procreation. And then I grew up in the sixties where women's liberation and sexual freedom became the new standards. I didn't adjust well. I was awkward and never had any girlfriends. I lost my virginity in 1973 when I was twenty-eight. I was at The Ting and a woman was very aggressive and I really didn't know how to respond. I just went along but it was hardly pleasant.

A few years later, I met Bev Smith and we became involved. Not long into the relationship, she became pregnant and Tegan was born. The three of us lived with the other guys in the house on Lenore. We never did get married. In fact, we never had a real relationship outside of having a daughter together, although we are quite friendly when we talk now. We moved as a unit to Calgary and it was there we stopped living together. She stayed in Calgary after I left, before she and Tegan moved to Montreal.

The only real relationship I have had has been with Emily, and I know it hasn't been easy for her. She says that I'm afraid of intimacy and I can't argue. I am. I grew up with a mother who wanted something else in life but settled for raising me with a husband that she didn't love in a country that was completely foreign. Some people overcome these things but I haven't.

I have had a lot of therapy over the years including Freudian psycho-therapy in my early twenties. My psychotherapist reduced everything to blaming my mother and it was of no use to me so I just quit going after a while. Not that my mother wasn't a complicated woman. Her art was the passion of her life and she would travel alone to Florida to paint by herself at a time where women of her age just didn't do such things. She was born into Russian aristocracy and lived a working-class life in Winnipeg. It would be naïve to think that these and other factors don't have some measure in making me into who I am. I also have a painting, hidden away, that she did of me that presents me as totally asymmetrical, almost hideous, and I guess I am left to wonder about that the rest of my life. Some of the therapists have been helpful, others not so much. Couples' therapy has helped Emily and me communicate better even though she is about her heart and emotion and I am more about my head and ideas. Being better with ideas and action is why I am so comfortable with politics.

Nick and his daughter, Tegan

Winnipeg in the late sixties and early seventies was also home to some fantastic theatre. One of my fondest memories was a visit by the San Francisco Mime Troupe who performed at the Playhouse Theatre. The play was called *Civil Rights in a Cracker Barrel*. It's still being performed and the troupe is still around. Somehow it got out that they were anarchists, and the buzz meant there could be a scene, which drew me in. I went to see the play and the players were all wearing blackface, like the vaudevillians. Nobody had a clue whether the actors were white or black. This is what the whole issue was. They wanted to demonstrate how people react to facial perspectives, whether or not we view somebody as an individual, or as a skin colour. And the way they demonstrated it was fascinating. In the intermission, instead of closing the curtain, they kept the stage open and they started to come off the stage inviting people to come up and dance with them. It was an interesting to watch how scared people were; only a few would go up on stage with them. Dancing with a black person? Now, we're talking about 1969, here. These boundaries were being crossed for the first time.

I also remember seeing John Coulter's play *The Trial of Louis Riel*. The reason I remember it is that I was late and by myself, so I had a seat in the front row. Before I knew it, I was part of the jury. Talk about being drawn into the story. I love theatre that is on the edge. I'm still a huge fan of our local Fringe Festival and try to support all the local companies as much as I can. There are lots of people in the performing arts community in Wolseley and I enjoyed having them as neighbours when we lived there.

True democratic reform is constantly being undermined. The Company of Young Canadians (CYC), Liberal Prime Minister Pierre Trudeau's creation, was a little like the Canadian version of the Peace Corps. I worked for the CYC, which paid an honorarium of two hundred dollars. I had a project of putting out an underground newspaper, a high school newspaper, for a little while and I was also doing some research work. There were a lot of unemployed young people that wanted to do something that mattered with their lives. They wanted to work in communities doing some community development, and Trudeau created the CYC in response. I think the intent was to take the radicalism out of the youth by channeling them into government programs — keep them engaged and buy into the system, even though it may not have succeeded in achieving this intention. The CYC worked from coast to coast doing community development work like tenant organizing, welfare rights advocacy and high school organizing. Some called this the "Children's Revolution" and Trudeau tried to buy off discontent by paying the two hundred dollar honorarium, which was peanuts even then, to do things so that they wouldn't go out and try to overthrow the government. Unfortunately for the government, the CYC became more of a radical organization than they had planned.

One of the workers I remember was Joe Bova, who was a founder of Manshield Construction and one of the most successful land developers Winnipeg has ever seen. He was prominent in the Liberal Party and well known for philanthropy. But he was also a member of the CYC with me. He was the perfect success story that Trudeau was looking for. I remind him where he came from when I see him and he's never happy when I do. I tell him the CYC was a revolutionary group — even if Trudeau didn't intend for it to turn out that way. I'd love to see the list of former members from coast to coast. I am pretty sure we all would be surprised by a few of the names that would crop up. I ended up being fired from the CYC because I took off from my work to attend the national New Democratic convention to support James Laxer. I ended up staying at his father's house. *Red Diapers* is the name of the book where Laxer tells the story of his communist upbringing in the home of Robert Laxer. I liked being in the house. A few years ago Laxer spoke at Mondragon Bookstore and Coffee House and I went to reconnect with him and CBC ended up filming us together for television.

Another part of the scene of the late sixties and early seventies was the election of the first NDP government in Manitoba — in 1969. I can't argue against the fact that it was that government that funded some community organizing groups that enabled me to be involved. However, it was also the beginning of the end of the NDP as a real socialist party. The move to the middle, conservative territory has defined the party ever since. Mel Watkins described the Waffle movement perfectly when he said it was "too weak to win and too strong to be tolerated."

The history of the Waffle movement is short. The Waffle Manifesto was delivered in 1969, and by 1972 Stephen Lewis engineered a resolution to disband the Waffle group within the Ontario NDP. The Manitoba Young New Democrats were a truly socialist group and many of us supported James Laxer when he ran for National Leader at the 1971 convention in Ottawa. The Manitoba Young New Democrats had a huge part in shaping who I am. We had held forums with very talented and knowledgeable people. Our space for the forums was at 256 Langside, across the street from where the Liberal Party now has their offices. It was actually the home of Russ Rothney, who manages community economic development with the Assiniboine Credit Union. He and his wife provided a mass of books to borrow and opened up their basement for people to gather and listen to talks. Ken Hanly, Harold Thimm, Sundhir Joshi and Ron Fletcher were some of the people we had giving talks. Many left the party. The MYND chapter at the University of Winnipeg folded in protest of the centrist positioning of the party. I stayed for many more years until Howard Pawley called me a racist when I spoke out about ethnic recruiting in the NDP. That was the final straw and I let my membership lapse, never to join any party again.

In the sixties, the committed leftists were all about ideology. The ideology was very heavy and they just didn't believe in what they called reformism. The left was dismissive of anyone who worked to change social institutions. They claimed they were there to create a socialist and then a communist society. A revolution was necessary and people were talking about taking a gun and shooting the capitalists. This one-track thinking made it hard to work with groups that were full of Marxists, Trotskyites and Maoists. How do you respond to ideas like that? Even Lenin said it was right to participate in parliament in a capitalist country.

During the FLQ crisis, there were posters with people standing on the corner with guns in their hands. Looking back, it was insane. This is maybe

"Last of the Red Hot Socialists" by Tom Andrich

why the first ten years of my life were so important. I knew the cost of war and the cost of guns from birth. In fact, it is all I knew. I believed in a socialist society then and I still do. I just don't think an armed struggle is going to bring it about.

We also have to remember that violence is not all physical. There is a lot of psychological violence and a lot of mental violence and even spiritual violence. Guns aren't needed to violate people and a narrow definition of violence prevents us from seeing the violence in front of us for what it is.

Capitalism functions in a violent way. Capitalism is violent in and of itself. That is part of the reason it would be a lie for me to say I am a non-violent person or a pacifist. If I participate in the violent system of capitalism, which I do, then I am violent myself. If you attack me, I am going to defend myself. One year I was going to work for the Mennonite Central Committee and I answered all their questions correctly except for the question asking if I was a pacifist. I wasn't hired. They were very clear. You had to state you were a pacifist in order to work for the Mennonite Central Committee. It was a chance for me to be honest about who I was and who I am.

Don't get me wrong, though, I was never going to use a gun to make my political points and I never will. I'm not a terrorist, I never was a terrorist and I never will be a terrorist. Many terrorists are apolitical anarchists creating violence for the sake of violence; their motto is "destroy and something good will come of it." Police agents tend to foster such ideas. Terrorism is counter-revolutionary because it plays into the hands of governments who want to prevent progressive movements from achieving a base.

I thought that the Weathermen, a radical student group out of the U.S. who blew up government buildings and banks, was wasting time, energy and lives. In the seventies, I paid attention to Germany, where some of the radicals decided they were going to make the revolution because the population as a whole was not ready to make it. This didn't make sense to me. A revolution will only come when the majority of people are ready to make a revolution. I go the Mondragon Bookstore and Coffeehouse where the young anarchists meet and hear them say, "You know, we're going to make the revolution," and I know I have nothing to teach them. The truth or non-truth of that idea has to be discovered. It isn't something that one can argue or teach. At some point, it requires personal experience. People have to travel their own road in order to arrive at their own understandings.

At one point, I thought that we, the elder generation, should be able to go to these young twenty-somethings and say, "Hey, we did this, and this was wrong, you should learn from us and you should..." but it just doesn't work that way! The only way people change is through living a vulnerable life, so that their choices have an impact on them.

Teaching means leading and encouraging people through those experiences, not trying to help them avoid those experiences. That is why I continue to say, "The more things change, the more they stay the same." It is one of my favourite quotations. You can find it in George Bernard Shaw's *Revolutionist's Handbook*, published in 1903. Every generation is going to complain about the younger generation. It has to be that way. Marx called this the dialectic force. It can't be shortcut. This doesn't mean I won't talk about my experiences. I can share them, but I can't tell somebody, "Don't make the mistakes I made." This also explains why people drop out. Very few people who I worked with in the sixties are still out there working for change. I haven't got a clue what's happened to them and I am not going to go onto Facebook to try to find them. Sadly, given my health, my time is very precious. I think they left the movement because they never went through enough experiences of their own to say, "Hey, this is something that is going to make my life relevant to me." They wound up accepting the system and living comfortably within in it. I understand that. I don't get upset about it. It is true for each generation.

I've met people that got involved in the movement for change in the eighties that are not active today. I've known people who got active in the nineties and are not active today. It takes time to be active. When people decide they no longer have the time, they stop being activists and we don't have change. I am a Marxist in the sense that I accept the dialectic of Marxism, which Marx talked about — you move from feudalism to capitalism, from capitalism to socialism and from socialism, ultimately, to communism. I reject the rhetoric that socialism has failed and capitalism has triumphed. We're a long way from any concept of a socialist state; there is no country that is truly socialist. There are countries that have elements of socialism, including Cuba, but I don't really consider Cuba to be overtly socialist. I mean, it's got aspects that I don't think are really socialist, but I understand.

In 1917, I would have become a Menshevik rather than a Bolshevik. Martov, who was one of the leaders of the Mensheviks, felt that you couldn't create socialism out of feudalism, which is what Lenin and even Stalin wound up trying to do. You can't jump historically from a feudalistic country to a socialist or communist country. Russia was not a capitalist country in 1917. Stalin created a state capitalism. Even Lenin admitted that the Soviet Union was in transition between capitalism and socialism, and he used the words "state capitalist" in 1921 and Stalin solidified it. He thought state capitalism was advancement over capitalism and that it ultimately would evolve into socialism, but that didn't happen. Martov and others said that socialism could only come from an advanced, and not a state, capitalism. When Stalinism collapsed and the Soviet Union followed in the late eighties and early nineties, the people realized that state capitalism could not provide the basic means for the average person.

Millions of people wound up on the street refusing to participate in the political system, and the system collapsed. There wasn't that much violence there. I think that's what's going to happen to capitalism. It may take another hundred years, but I just believe that, ultimately, capitalism will fail. Likely, this will be for ecological reasons alone. We're going to run out of oil reserves, and we're going to run out of other resources, so we're going to have to live more simply, more "green," if you want to call it that, on a very large scale. It will be an entirely different way of being. Ultimately, you can't keep on producing and producing and making money.

In the next twenty to thirty years, there will be no energy, no oil or gasoline — only electricity (as it is renewable) and heating and cooling by solar energy. There will be no cars and no big box developments. What do you do then? James Howard Kunstler, in his book *The Long Emergency*, suggests that cities' population will be depleted, suburbia will collapse and people will move into the centre of the city using the resources there in order to survive. Roads will have to be transformed into pedestrian walkways and bicycle paths, while the public transportation system will consist of electric railways (light railway transit). With the loss of big box merchandisers, large farms will collapse and we will have to learn how to grow our own food. Cities will literally be transformed into village-like structures — much like the old days.

Personally, I can't imagine all this will unfold logically and peacefully. The middle class and others who benefit from the way things are today will not give up quietly. There will be crisis, chaos and possibly revolution. It is not far-fetched to imagine a form of fascism could arise with a leader telling people that they must live this way or they won't survive. We need to be vigilant in making sure that fascism does not emerge out of this crisis. As capitalism falls, those who benefit from it will cling to it at any cost. This battle may happen in this generation. Or, it may not.

There will be crises like those that we had in 1930. Capitalism nearly died in the early thirties. The only thing that saved capitalism during the economic crisis was the Second World War. We will get back to that place eventually because capitalism will not be able to continue to produce at the same level, and there will be a crisis. Maybe we are in it even as I write. People will simply say, "Capitalism doesn't take care of our needs." People will stand up in the streets and the majority will truly be the majority.

Ultimately, the new women's movement, the ecological movement, the Aboriginal movement, the poor people's movement — the politics of the personal — emerged from the 1960s, from our lives, our work and our culture. We ought not to forget nor deny this reality.

6

Democracy

"If I had to sum up my life I might say I simply wanted to make a point … A democracy is central to making that point."

My first arrest occurred in 1970. The circumstances were documented in a movie called *Festival Express*. Janis Joplin, The Grateful Dead, The Band and others were travelling across Canada by train and playing concerts at all the major centres. The completed documentary film was released in 2003.

It cost twelve dollars to attend the Festival Express stop in Winnipeg, so there was a bunch of us who gathered and went to protest, chanting, "Make it free! Make it free!" It was far from my number one issue, in part because I preferred Pete Seeger and Phil Ochs to Joplin, The Dead and The Band. I didn't really need to see the music, but I was there. I ended up with a bullhorn in my hand. There were three or four hundred students, and all kinds of hippies and whoever else, just ready to do something. Only a few of them were my friends. I knew them from the MYND wing but the rest were not politically active. All of a sudden, we were surrounded by the police. This was only about six weeks after the National Guard had killed four students in a protest at Kent State University in Ohio.

The Red River Exhibition was on outside the stadium where the concert was being held. Eventually I left for a break and wandered through the "Ex." When I came back, there were only fifty or sixty of the demonstrators left outside the stadium and they were marching. I still had the bullhorn, so I wound up in the lead. At this point, there were almost as many police as there were protesters, so the cops were a little cockier than they had been earlier. I may have been mouthy but I know that I never touched a single police officer. It was tense but not explosive. Then, around midnight, word spread that The Grateful Dead had come out of the venues and played for demonstrations in other cities, so we began to think they would come out and give us a free show. The cops realized that if the entire crowd poured out with them, things could get worse in a hurry, so they decided to form a massive line and start pushing everybody back. Everybody except me! They pushed me behind their line and pushed everybody else out of the way. Then they dragged me away from the crowd and beat the shit out of me. It was all pretty quick but there were two distinct parts. First, it was the uniformed police who dragged me away and then it was plainclothes officers who beat me with several body shots using their fists. They thought no one could see them but luckily there were witnesses. The officers knew how to beat me in such a way that there was no physical evidence. Back in those days, there were no cell phones to capture what happened.

Then they took me to the drunk tank at the Public Safety Building and charged me with assaulting a police officer. This was the one and only time I ever was in a drunk tank, as I drink very little and was not drinking that night. I didn't realize where I was until they told me as I was leaving to go home. It made sense, as there was absolutely nothing in the room — not even a mattress. I was the only one there. They had taken everything away from me. They told me they were preventing me from committing suicide. I was trying to sleep and you can't sleep on a cold floor, especially if you have not been drinking.

The next morning, my friend Lawrie Cherniack came and bailed me out for about a hundred dollars. When they released me, I went to a doctor and he found a few bruises and took pictures, but nothing came of it. Nobody even knew that I had been arrested. It was midnight when it all happened and the media had left the demonstration. Nobody was around. After a few days, my friends in the MYND were ready to take this case seriously. Police brutality was, and is, a real issue.

Cy Gonick, who had been elected to the legislature with an NDP win in 1969, raised the issue of police brutality in the legislature, using my case as an example. Mitch Podolak had asked him to do that and it got some results. All of a sudden police investigators showed up at my door wanting to know the whole story. We had done some homework already and had tracked down the witnesses. We showed the investigators how the officers beat me up when they arrested me and reiterated that I had not done anything illegal. Since it had been a legal demonstration, eventually the charges against me were stayed. Assaulting a police officer is a very serious charge and I could only have feared the worst had I been convicted.

For Nick it was always about democracy

Knowing that the truth would eventually have to come out, we decided that we would go to the Police Commission and request a hearing into the conduct of the officers who beat me, and that is when my case became public. It seemed like my name was in the headlines every day in 1971. Ironically, it was a man who would later become the Attorney General who came and asked to be my lawyer. Roland Penner, who was working with Joe Zuken, approached me about the case; I was delighted to have a man of his talent and commitment to represent me. The case was mine but it was a project of the entire MYND wing, who thought this was the right battle to fight. Even though Penner had been raised as a communist, he was the voice of calm and reason beside the youth wing, who wanted him to take a more radical, militant and oppositional position in the hearing. The MYND was very good at getting people to the courtroom, so every time I appeared the place was packed with supporters.

This is when I learned the power of the media and how they can destroy you. This is also how I first met the CJOB Radio talk show host Peter Warren, because he attacked me on his radio show. He said I was nothing but a "communist troublemaker, wanting to overthrow the government." Even though my charges had been dropped, he labelled me a criminal. The left tended to ignore the media and I did too, but I saw the power of the press and realized I was forsaking it to my own peril. This was a life-changing moment: I seized upon the available media, doing interviews and writing letters whenever and wherever I could. Only now is it clear how that cost me. The constant exposure in the papers and on TV and radio at that time made it impossible for me to find work. Everybody knew me from that incident and they didn't want to touch me. Media was so different then. Winnipeggers at the time read papers, listened to the radio and watched TV. They knew what was in the news. An hour on Peter Warren's show really got you in people's faces. Or in their ears, at least.

In the end, the case lost four to one at the Police Commission. They found the police actions to be appropriate. Even the one vote in my favour came from someone making a point about the police administration, not about what happened.

In early 1982, Bob Bragg, a *Calgary Herald* reporter, approached about a half dozen of us radicals telling us that new legislation was to be introduced in Ottawa on personal privacy and freedom of information. The *Calgary Herald* wanted to find out whether we could get access to information concerning files that the RCMP had maintained on us and they wanted us to apply for these files. Five of us did apply and the RCMP denied us all. Of those, four didn't want to go on with it, but not me — having raised the importance of freedom of information many times in the past, I was determined to test the RCMP's power to make such denials. I took the RCMP to court and represented myself with some minor successes with motions. Sheldon Chumir, a well-known Calgary lawyer with an interest in civil liberties, contacted me during that time. He told me up front that he had no interest in payment. I was thrilled. From 1982 until late in 1991, he represented me without any fees. Tragically, he died in early 1992, just before my final day in court. We were still fighting when he took sick, though he was able to celebrate with me when we received a significant number of documents in 1987.

By the end of my legal actions, I had received over four hundred and fifty pages of RCMP files about me. There was a lot blacked out, but I could read between the lines. The RCMP named me as a terrorist and a subversive. Later they had to acknowledge that this wasn't true and that I was only a lawful advocate, protester and dissenter. Who knows how many thousands of dollars were spent following me around? Peter Warren loved the story. He knew I was no threat to our country's safety. In fact, I eventually helped him recover the files they had kept on *him*!

The civil liberties community was generally more interested in my freedom of information case than the left ever was. My files included an entire transcription of a TV show I was on where CJAY-TV host Ray Torgrud interviewed me and I talked about Jesus being a communist. It was aired at ten in the morning on Boxing Day. I am not sure if I ever met anyone who actually watched it! I spoke of Jesus as a man of the poor, fighting for the poor. The RCMP appended a three-page analysis to the transcript. It accused me of being a terrorist, a communist and a threat to religion. They were also suspicious of Ray Torgrud, who was actually a libertarian — a follower of Ayn Rand — just because he and I were friends. It is important for people to know that our government spent a lot of money on stupid commentaries written by people who had no idea what politics was all about — people who didn't even know the left from the right or anything in between!

There are still two hundred to two hundred and fifty pages they tell me are of too much importance to national security to ever be released. I suspect that material relates to people in the Communist Party and others I knew — people they thought were even more dangerous than I am. The blacked-out parts of what I did get seemed to be protecting the identity of the RCMP spies. Most of my file was public record, newspaper clippings and the like, but clearly they had people writing things down at meetings, some of which were public, some not so public. It is also clear that they tapped my phone at some point because there are specific details about conversations I had only on my phone. They even lost me once! I was working in a northern Aboriginal community and there are notes that read, "Where's Ternette, we have to track him down!" I wasn't hiding. I was working on a reserve in Saskatchewan. Everyone who knew me knew that. They paid all those officers high wages to be incredibly inept. They even quote washroom graffiti in my file. They certainly left no stone unturned!

They admit to having maintained a file starting in 1966. I received my files covering 1966 to 1983. They wouldn't give me anything after 1983 and I haven't asked for any files since then. The government paranoia peaked in 1970. The FLQ crisis had everybody on edge but I expect I am still officially considered to be a terrorist and a subversive. It is both sad and ironically funny that the government had this interest in me, but there were real implications to the way they played up my politically subversive persona. For example, in 1969, I was coaching football and baseball at the West End

Memorial Community Club. John Mark, the community club recreation supervisor, pulled me aside and said, "You know what? The police came here in uniform and they were asking questions about you." He then explained that the police thought that I should not be coaching the kids because I was a communist. I guess the cop actually said I was influencing these kids to become communists in the future and because of that, the centre should fire me. I should be fired as a volunteer coach because I was a communist? This was not the U.S. in the McCarthy era, this was Winnipeg in the seventies! Mark knew I didn't talk politics with the kids, so he told the officer to go to hell, but when he told me the story, it made me want to quit coaching.

My political persona as a subversive found its way into other areas of my life, when a similar thing happened at the German-Canadian Club. Jack Thiessen, a right-wing professor of German at the University of Winnipeg, made it his business to oppose me. Eventually he had me banned from our local German-Canadian Club — where I socialized with other people with German backgrounds — as a communist, even though he couldn't even manage to get my political persona right. For that, I called him a Nazi and we had many battles over the years. He wrote a number of nasty letters to the editor and I didn't hold back much when I had the chance to respond. The same organization was quite unhappy with me when, later, I opposed the idea of putting up a piece of the Berlin Wall at the Forks and locating a German-Canadian Club near it. I thought the wall was a point of shame for Germans and did not need to be displayed, and that the Forks is clearly a place for us to honour Aboriginal history and land that we live in and I did not want to detract from that either.

Around the same time, during the FLQ crisis, the police picked me up on Portage Avenue. They were in an unmarked car. They weren't arresting me; they just pushed me in the car and said they wanted to talk. We drove along Portage Avenue for several blocks. They didn't have questions, they just had a message. "Don't lead a revolution here in Winnipeg!" All I could do was laugh because I knew we had no insurrection coming in this country. Sure, some of the local Maoists were putting up posters with pictures declaring violence as a means of political change, but we were a long way away from overthrowing the (NDP) government in Manitoba. I told them that the people who put up the posters didn't even know which end of a gun to hold on to, but the officers were dead serious. They had a job to do and that was to intimidate little Nick and get him away from influencing the youth. Seeing as I gave up coaching about that time, I guess they got their way.

In a 1972 document, the RCMP reported, "Mr. Ternette" had "very little influence on students at the University of Winnipeg." Another RCMP report concludes that, "it is felt that Ternette is intelligent enough to realize that in order to achieve his political aims, it will have to be done through a bona fide political party, namely the NDP, an organization that has provided him with considerable assistance in the past." Furthermore, another report stated that I was "a card-carrying NDP member during [my] candidacy in the 1971 municipal election in Winnipeg." This was classified under "General conditions, subversive activities among revolutionary youth — Canada General." This suggests that running for political office was, in the view of the RCMP, a subversive activity.

The Canadian Security Intelligence Service (CSIS) was created in 1984, in part I'm sure because of the ridiculous work the RCMP was doing trailing so-called revolutionaries. I am convinced my case was part of this development, because before 1984, there was a twenty-year wait after death before a person's files would be released. Tommy Douglas never saw his own files (they had a 1,142 page file on him). His family got the files twenty years after he died. Douglas always knew he was being followed and spied on. It is just that way in Canada. Anybody who went to the Ukrainian Labour Temple in the North End in the last one hundred years should have been ready to have his or her picture taken. No end of important political discussions happened in that building and I am sure we would all be blown away by the files that have been created and are sitting under lock and key in some CSIS building.

The *Globe & Mail* published a lead story when I received my surveillance files in 1987. I was living in Calgary during much of my freedom of information struggle, but I got more coverage nationally than I did in Winnipeg papers. Maybe they just didn't know how to write a story about me winning something!

This story is of great significance to Canadians. Although the RCMP would never admit to an actual number, estimates range between thirty thousand and several hundred thousand files on individual Canadians and organizations. An *Ottawa Citizen* article in 1985 says the RCMP had files on 1.5 million Canadians. Before I saw my file, no one else in the country was allowed to see theirs as it was considered a threat to national security. My friend Peter Warren wrote in a column that I had "gone where no man had gone before." The request form for access to such information is only a page long. Anyone can ask. Then the government has to prove you a bona fide threat in order to prevent a file's release.

I knew people everywhere and I guess following me gave them a lot of people to talk about. I had friends in the Trotskyist, Maoist and communist movements. I would be a moderator at some of their meetings. Tariq Ali, a world-renowned Pakistani critic of the Vietnam War and a member of a Trotskyist party, came to these meetings. Ernest Mandel, a German Marxist journalist of equal note, also came and I would be the master of ceremonies. We would have four hundred people show up for these things. As far as I was concerned, I was "the one and only" independent Marxist who refused to be aligned to any particular group, although others would argue that there were indeed unaligned Marxists. I think my independence didn't make sense to the police and they just assumed I was hiding something.

I did not and I still do not like sectarianism. I didn't like the in-fighting that happened. There would be a demonstration planned by the Maoists, and if the Maoists organized it then the Trots wouldn't participate; it was like that for everyone. They were all seemingly convinced that they each had the one true way figured out. At some level, it was not a lot different from the schisms of fundamentalist Christianity.

I tried to work with the Maoists — the Communist Party of Canada Marxist-Leninist — but it was very, very difficult. I would attend one of their meetings and I knew that the only people who would show up would be the Maoists, and unfortunately I wound up on the hanging list. Because of our ideological differences, they would say, "Ternette, you're a traitor to the revolution. The number one traitor in Winnipeg is Mitch Podolak. He will be hung first, and you're the number two traitor and you'll be hung second." Probably they told him I was number one and he was number two. They saw me as too moderate because I didn't believe in revolution that doesn't come from the people: as far as I am concerned, you don't make a revolution until the majority of people, or at least a significant minority, are ready to make serious change. Obviously, I couldn't work with them and although I eventually walked away, I was the last one to do so. Everyone else walked away before the Maoists even got started with them. I called them political cultists rather than a serious political movement.

I get along with them these days because they've changed their views not only about me but about everything. A lot of them were involved in SMAC (Structured Movements Against Capitalism). A lot of them are involved in the peace movement today, forty years later.

I thought I should be independent because I could reach more people that way. I had my own perspective and I didn't push it on anybody in particular. I felt it was important to be able to work with all kinds of people who weren't at the same political level, and it worked! I mean, that's why I know as many people as I do in this city. Even though I have always been at the far left of the political spectrum, I have always been able to talk to anyone. Some of my other connections may have gotten the eye of the RCMP. One of those was Dmitri Roussopoulos, who founded the peace journal *Our Generation,* which evolved into a libertarian, socialist and anarchist journal. Dmitri was part of the anarchist bookstore in Montreal that, in 1970, published *The New Left in Canada,* which includes my chapter on Manitoba. Out of all that grew Black Rose Books, which was one of Canada's most important leftist publishers.

Through Dmitri, I met Raya Dunayevskaya, who was Leon Trotsky's secretary in Mexico from 1938–1939. She had split with Trotsky — she called the Soviet Union state capitalist, while Trotsky called it a deformed workers' state. Less than a year later, in 1940, he was murdered in Mexico. After moving to the States, Raya wrote several books and is known for her trilogy of revolution. When I met her at a conference in Ottawa, she was teaching at Wayne State University in Detroit. I expect my being a German of Russian background drew her to me. She asked me to translate part of the *Grundrisse* of Karl Marx, which had never been translated, and I was so happy to be asked that I didn't admit that my German wasn't good enough to do that kind of work. So, I found a German professor at the University of Winnipeg who did take it on, and we did translate it. She liked the translation but it was never published because Martin Nicolaus, a Maoist in San Francisco, published his translation first. I met him too, at a conference in Toronto. It was the Year of the Barricades and we met at a demonstration against the *Globe & Mail.* The Students for a Democratic Society (SDS) in Germany sent people north from the States to the demonstration, and some Black Panthers were there too. Maybe the RCMP thought I would be helping to set up the Black Panthers in Winnipeg's North End.

My general feeling, looking back, is just disgust with the stupidity of the time, the energy and money they spent on me and who knows how many others. It was also an occasion for true national recognition for me as I had unprecedented media coverage for my victories in court. I take some satisfaction knowing that I inspired others to ask to see their files as well.

By 1992, I had received about half of my RCMP files and was refused as many as I received. I could not go on by myself because my lawyer, Sheldon Chumir, died of cancer. I had no resources to hire another lawyer and I wasn't going to go back to representing myself. Chumir's generosity was truly inspirational. He left a very large bequest when he died and now the Sheldon Chumir Foundation for Ethics in Leadership offers all sorts of support for justice and equality in the government and the private and not-for-profit sectors. My RCMP files are as much his story as they are my own. All his files are archived in Alberta, but because of attorney-client privilege there is a fifty-year waiting period. All my casework is there, with my name throughout it, but I can't access it. I do have everything that is released, but it would be interesting to see just what his files contain that I never heard about.

I continue to be a critic of the Winnipeg Police Service, but they are not really open to criticism. Even now they've been dragging their feet on implementing the civilian police commission. In forty years of activism, I have never seen the police do much more than twiddle with their public relations strategies. The municipal Standing Policy Committee on Protection and Community Services has never been effective, so having another group that reports to them is not likely to make a lot of difference. As an example, the Committee has never been able to ascertain from the police chief how effective the aggressive panhandling by-law is. It is arbitrary policing and the people of Winnipeg deserve better.

The Obstructive Solicitation By-law, which makes it illegal to beg at bank machines, credit unions, bus stops and so on (that is to say, anywhere there is considered to be a "captive" audience), was enacted under former mayor Susan Thompson in 1995. After years of struggle, the National Anti-Poverty Organization successfully challenged the constitutionality of that by-law in the Manitoba Court of Queen's Bench during Glen Murray's administration in 2000. This forced Murray to revise the by-law to become an aggressive panhandling by-law — that is, the basis for controlling panhandling would be the behaviour of panhandlers rather than their location. This change made the by-law even more difficult for the police to enforce.

No one really knows why Mayor Sam Katz revised it again and consolidated it in 2005 to become the Obstructive Solicitation By-law, which in essence was the same by-law that was enacted under Thompson. Even though former police chief Jack Ewatski indicated to city council that there was about a charge a week under this by-law, no one is ready to tell how many have appeared in court, how many were fined, or how many have possibly gone to jail. No question, panhandling and anti-squeegee by-laws are meant to make those individuals disappear from sight — out of sight, out of mind. And while two decades ago the Supreme Court ruled that panhandling is freedom of speech, it also ruled that cities can regulate panhandling. We do not have absolute freedom of speech in this country; freedom of speech can be and is regulated. The question that the Supreme Court will have to determine is, "Who are the panhandlers?" Are they buskers, who entertain for the money you give them, people who sit or stand with their hat in their hand or addicts (who, in my opinion are not panhandlers)? Furthermore, the court will need to determine whether a by-law based on behaviour is too restrictive or whether a by-law based on location is too restrictive — or both.

A related issue is putting signs on hydro poles and other public places. I spoke to city council about their arbitrary approach of setting a limit on the number of kiosks and designating certain poles for posters. This is a basic freedom of speech issue and one that Mitch Podoluk should get the credit for. We are able to poster in this city for musical, political, community and other events because of his determination in preventing efforts by the city to suppress this type of communication.

Only now, in 2012, is our city working towards a new civilian police board, which will meet behind closed doors instead of being open to the public. City Counsellor Dan Vandal pointed out that the board will not oversee police department budgets, staffing levels, labour relations in general or even the hiring of a police chief. In my opinion, the board will consist of puppets. It is highly unlikely that they will probe police misconduct cases with any seriousness. The horrific stories of the last few years are waking up the public a little, but it seems most people are generally apathetic in accepting the state of our police service. Even in ever-conservative Alberta,

Edmonton puts us to shame in the way they hold their police accountable to the public.

One of the key principles of civilian oversight of the police service is to de-politicize police decision making. The police must operate independently and without influence or even appearance of influence over enforcing the law, while at the same time being accountable to the public for fiscal or operational matters. Why is it that cities all across Canada, except Winnipeg, have recognized the importance of establishing arm's-length civilian police commissions in order to provide a balance of police independence, on the one hand, and public accountability on the other? For example, if we had a civilian police commission, would the chief be able to challenge Mayor Sam Katz on his approach to addressing crime?

Our city requires policing based on decisions grounded in good public policy under the direction of an independent and arm's-length police commission. The status quo approach to police governance in Winnipeg lacks accountability and is ineffective. We need a police commission with more than simply an advisory role.

Even more important to me is the fact that the agency that presently deals with police misconduct is not accountable to anyone. Isn't it obvious that the Law Enforcement Review Agency (LERA) officers are in a conflict of interest when they have to return to regular police work after investigating officers in their LERA role?

While police used to intimidate protest groups through criminal charges, they have a new weapon now: the provincial *Highway Traffic Act*. They are using psychological intimidation with groups like Critical Mass, which holds a cycling event on the last Friday of each month in over three hundred cities worldwide. The point of the event is to get large numbers of cyclists on main roads at the same time to disrupt traffic and show that our roadways aren't properly designed to handle bike traffic. It is a great form of civil disobedience. It makes the need to do something differently patently obvious, but, in Winnipeg, the police shut it down by harassing demonstrators with traffic violations and an inordinately large police presence. I knew a lot of the Critical Mass protestors; some were young anarchists I met at Mondragon Bookstore and Coffeehouse and others were neighbours from Wolseley. The police wanted to have discussions with the Critical Mass leaders, but they did not understand collective anarchism.

Critical Mass was not interested in being co-opted with false dialogue but rather in disrupting the status quo so change had to happen. People who might be attending a demonstration for the first time would most certainly be deterred from participating in even more demonstrations. There have been some changes in the city to improve biking, such as the creation of new bike lanes, but we have a long way to go before cycling is a true option for commuting. The shutdown of the Critical Mass group was an abuse of the *Highway Traffic Act*, the purpose of which is public safety not the prevention of peaceful protest.

It is not just encounters with the police that demonstrate the limits of our democracy. I was part of the Centennial Residents' Advisory Group from 1972 to 1975 and eventually chaired the group. This was an unprecedented experiment in participatory democracy and we could get a hundred local residents out to a meeting to discuss the issues that mattered locally. It was part of the Unicity initiative. It died out because as the groups became more aware, they wanted more power to act rather than just provide advice, and when the power to enact change didn't come, people became disenchanted. Once the Conservatives got back in, they claimed there was "disinterest" in the program; today it is only a shadow of what it was. There had been a wonderful vision articulated in the white paper authored by Meyer Brownstone, who, among other things, won the Pearson Medal for Peace and served as chair of Oxfam. His vision had the Resident Advisory Groups (RAGs) as the key element in a system of participatory democracy, where they would actually become the true instrument of government. His dream was turned completely on its head and was never achieved. The professional politicians had far too much at stake to allow such radical ideas to restructure the very culture of city council.

Another fight in my life was in 1977 when I claimed, in an application to the Human Rights Commission of Manitoba, that my political views were being used against me when I applied for jobs in non-political realms. I was applying for positions all over the country without success. I kept all my rejection letters and they made a huge stack. These were not blanket applications. I was applying for work in youth leadership, communications, the environment and administration, and I had extensive experience in all those areas. I went to the Human Rights Commission, which ruled that they could not deal with the issue and forced the hand of Howard Pawley and the provincial government to change the *Human Rights Act* to protect against discrimination on the basis of political views and belief systems. The Ombudsman said that without a definition of a "political belief system" no claim could be made. The government responded by basing their definition of "political" on membership in a particular political party. Simply holding political views — in my case, being a Marxist — was not enough. The accepted definition was too narrow to be of any use to me and, no doubt, to many others. It was only later, in 1983, that they broadened the understanding of "political" to include political activities in general.

I would never take any perverse pride in simply making work for others, but the Human Rights Commission undertook extensive investigations into local hiring practices as a result of my complaint to them. The Commission questioned both the City of Winnipeg, which I challenged for hiring people who were less qualified than I was into social work jobs, and a non-profit organization called Citizen Advisory Inc. In late 1977, Citizen Advisory Inc., where I was to do staff coordination, public relations and volunteer training, actually told me I had a job and then "un-hired" me the following day when some board members heard of the offer and wanted no part of me. I had already been given the office keys! When I looked at the paperwork, it was clear to me that a lot of backpedalling was going on. In one of the reports I am quoted as saying "I know I am a shit-disturber," which they used against me to say it was the style not the substance of my politics that was at issue. For a true radical, political style and substance are inseparable, and to this day, I stand by my claims. In a private sense this is simply another "loss" I suffered as a result of my politics. I was not given the job and continued for the rest of my working life to face similar discrimination to the point where I really gave up trying. I do have a sense of victory that Manitobans now have protection from human rights abuses related to political associations and activities. My six years (1977–1983) of letter writing and all the related pushing and shoving were far from wasted.

In spite of all the screaming I have done to promote our democratic rights, I still have trouble getting my head around how apathetic the voter population is. With little exception, there has been a continuous decline in voting. The long-term danger is that, in future, we will accept a less than fifty per cent voter turnout as normal. In the 2006 city election, the councillors who ran had served, on average, twelve years. At least two, councillors

Harry Lazarenko and Mike O'Shaughnessy, had been elected for the first time over thirty years prior to that election. No question, term limits would have an impact on the re-election of city councillors and provide some fresh blood in the civic process. When Susan Thompson was mayor she initiated the investigation that led to the Cuff Report. The implementation of that report has fundamentally altered the structure of city government by centralizing political power into the Executive Policy Committee, which is not accountable to the public, sets its own agendas and holds secret meetings to ensure there is a degree of consensus among members before any major issue comes forth for public debate. What we have today is cabinet-style government at city hall without accountability.

In contrast, the provincial government, and most other provincial governments in Canada, allow public hearings on all bills presented in the legislature. Unfortunately, the manner in which these public hearings are held is a concern to both the politicians and the public. Quite bluntly, waiting six hours to be heard is quite a "challenge." As many presenters, including myself, have said, there have to be better mechanisms put in place for democracy in action. As I suggested, maybe rural delegations should be heard in their own communities and Winnipeg delegations heard here in the city. Unfortunately, while the rules stated that delegations had ten minutes to make their presentations and five minutes for questions and discussion, some delegations were more equal than others.

Concerning the *Election Finances Amendment Act*, labour activists and I supported public financing of political campaigns as opposed to private donations to political parties. At the time, I strongly argued that an amendment is required to determine what defines a registered political party, in that the Communist Party had been deregistered at the federal level because it did not have fifty candidates. Manitoba requires five candidates running in order to have a registered political party. In a 2003 court challenge under the *Charter of Rights and Freedoms*, the Supreme Court threw out the law requiring fifty candidates in a party and ruled that one candidate is sufficient for a party to be considered registered; though in Manitoba five candidates are still required.

The more public financing there is, the more political parties there will be to participate in the electoral process, giving voters a greater range of "ideas." I also believe that further legislation is required concerning the

Elections Act if we are to advance democracy; we should lower the voting age to sixteen from eighteen and bring in proportional representation, which has already been considered in other provinces.

During budget debates at city hall in 2006, I was the only citizen who went to city hall to make a comment and I was met with a room full of glassy-eyed councillors. Bill Clement even fell asleep. The press was happy to report on this but not being listened to had become something I was quite used to. Very recently I was there to talk about issues related to buses and the disabled. Now that I am a double amputee elder statesman, I noticed they were actually listening. This image of me being "the only one there" was one picked up by my friend Rodney Graham, who founded *Street Sheet Canada*, a newspaper that began in defence of the squeegee kids. Rodney summed me up in an article as the one who was "willing to stand alone" and be the movement all by myself if needed.

One of the strikes against me as a proponent of democracy, maybe the only one, was when City Councillor Jae Eadie said that I refused to submit expense forms for my campaigns. For the record, I never broke the law as Eadie suggested. When the *Finances Act* was introduced in 1992, I ran for city council knowing that I would not be able to run for office again until I filed an audited statement, which I did in 1994 so that I could run for mayor in 1995. I did not file an audited statement after my campaign in 1995, knowing that I could not run for council or mayor in 1998, a year in which I ran for school board. In 2002, my twentieth election, I didn't file an audited statement because I had decided that it was my final time running for office. It seemed crazy for me to pay an auditor four hundred dollars or more for the short list of people who gave me donations that might be little more than that amount in total. It makes sense if someone is elected that they be accountable for who supported them, but for those who are not elected, what difference does it make? In my opinion, Eadie supported the submitting of expense claims to close off the electoral process and keep it in the hands of the rich. He had other initiatives, such as increased filing fees, to reach the same ends. Fringe candidates in and of themselves threaten those in power. To me, preventing the fringe candidate, or making it difficult for them to participate, undermines democracy. No one has ever been charged under these municipal election financing laws because they know how foolish the laws are if enforced, but we do not know how foolish they are in preventing good men and women from entering the political world and offering their names for public service.

Since the Winnipeg General Strike of 1919, the CCF/NDP have been heavily involved in civic politics. The inability of the NDP to reach beyond the inner city of Winnipeg has left Winnipeg civic politics in a quandary. Some candidates run as Independents when, in fact they are members of the NDP or even the Green Party, but they want to catch some of the Liberal or maybe some of the Tory vote. This practice encourages confusion and leads candidates to reflect centrist

Nick speaking at a demonstration at Winnipeg City Hall

politics, leaving scant ideological differences between them. It also forces the worst kind of politics, where people vote for the "lesser of the evils" based on personalities, not politics. This is the dismal history of Winnipeg City Council.

While I have collected my thoughts here on democracy, I do not mean to imply that democracy is an issue unto itself. Democratic process and personal authority and autonomy are reflected in every aspect of our lives. For instance, income issues are also at the core of what democracy means to me. Guaranteed annual income, for example, is not just a cause of the left. It is cost-effective, so those on the right who have done their homework like it too. But, it is a hard political sell because it seems to be "giving something for nothing." In the 1980s the federal Forget Inquiry, the Ryan Task Force and the federal Macdonald Commission made recommendations towards guaranteed annual income programs. I made some noise whenever the chance arose but I wasn't surprised the governments of the day did not go anywhere with the recommendations. Since then, guaranteed annual income seems to get only the rarest of consideration.

Education has always been a central concern in my life, as it is a core principle of democracy since decision making needs to be informed. On top of teaching upgrading classes when I was young and organizing conferences such as the Youth and Delinquency Conference, which I chaired in at the University of Winnipeg 1967, and the Free University experiment a few years later, I was involved in several different ventures into free public education. In the late 1980s I was part of the Winnipeg Socialist Education Centre. Kent Gerecke and I offered a course in Green Politics. Alden Turner, an English professor, offered a course on the Rhetoric of Rock, and the Bread and Roses Collective put on a series on Socialist Feminism. Jim Silver, at the University of Winnipeg, and Wayne Antony, then a part-time lecturer at the University of Winnipeg, were the driving forces behind this effort.

If I had to sum up my life I might say I simply wanted to make a point. There is a way to look at alternatives to capitalism. There are options. We don't have to accept it and all its problems. A democracy is central to making that point. Democracy requires involvement and almost everything I have done in my life can be understood as promoting that reality. Most of what I have done is simply trying to be engaged: offering input and speaking out about the various nefarious ways in which our participation in democracy is not encouraged but rather discouraged by those with power.

7

"If I Were Mayor of Winnipeg"

"Nick Ternette's Winnipeg wouldn't have allowed developers to scuttle true planning for their own gains."

Not long ago, somebody asked me what I thought Winnipeg would look like if I had won the mayor's seat back when I first ran in 1977 and held the office until 2002 when I ran for the last time. All I could do was laugh. The election results are a matter of public record and the highest I ever placed was third and that was thousands and thousands of votes behind the winner. But, as a hypothetical question, it is maybe something that every Winnipegger might wish to ask. What would the city be like if you were mayor?

Maybe the most visible difference would be the absence of a great big underused railway yard separating north from south in our city. The development of this area has been on the agenda (way at the bottom) for a long time and likely will remain there. The Canadian Pacific Railway yards have always defined our city. Even recently, Pat Martin, NDP MP for Winnipeg Centre, has talked actively about moving them. Greg Selinger wrote his PhD dissertation on the yards.

This is not my idea but I think I have a relatively distinct take on the importance of such a move. When it does finally happen, it will put an end to that great break and free up space for new residential housing in the urban core. You can't find many cities that are still cut in half by a railway. It is bad for the environment. It is bad for transportation. It is bad for community. It is just plain bad. I have spoken out about relocating the railways every decade since the seventies, but it continues to look like government will never put forth the millions that such a move would require. But it would be worth it and it will never get any cheaper to do that kind of excavation. We should have relocated the yard forty years ago but that doesn't mean it wouldn't be the right thing to do now. The railway was central in Winnipeg in the 1920s but since the building of the Panama Canal, those freight yards are like a beacon signalling that we are a hundred years behind the times. It is no lie to say Winnipeg never recovered from the opening of the Panama Canal.

When my father came to Winnipeg, he came by rail. Bus service was minimal and airplanes were too expensive. Everybody went by train. Winnipeg's only true period of growth, known as the "Chicago Era," was from 1900 to 1920. We were going to become the Chicago of the North, and the railway was at the centre of this destiny. Even in 1955, my father was getting work on an extra gang (a group of workers who are not assigned to maintain a certain section of track but are sent where and when needed). Trains went south to the States, through Minneapolis and Chicago too.

The Hudson's Bay and Eaton's department stores were built in and around that growth period and they defined our downtown. But with the growth never being followed up, our downtown has no definition. Those who don't know Winnipeg's vibrant downtown of the sixties, particularly Portage Avenue between the two stores, don't know how bad our downtown really is today. It is like a ghost in comparison. If you look at the same downtown section right now, you have the MTS Centre on the site of Eaton's, which is empty all day every day, and a Bay store with half the floors empty and very few customers on the floors that are open.

Had we relocated the yards a generation ago, all that new urban core housing could have supported a vibrant downtown, not only making downtown more accessible to the North End, but changing the entire culture of the city. You can say that what separates north from south in Winnipeg is the Assiniboine River or Portage Avenue but the real divide is the railway yards. Thirty or forty years without them would have gone a long way to challenge the parochialism of our city. While housing and the retail needed to support housing could have been the primary use of that land, green space, dedicated recreation centres and other uses could have transformed what currently is little more than a big empty hole.

Relocating the rail yards should have happened during the debate over the building of the MacGregor Street overpass. The Pawley Government won the provincial election for the NDP in 1981, and while the Conservatives were prepared to build this bridge, the premier called a moratorium on construction. The campaigns for and against building it had started in 1970 and did not finish until more than ten years later. This is one of the issues where I thought that Joe Zuken was on the wrong side by supporting the overpass, because North Enders wanted and needed a way to get downtown. Going back to the aftermath of 1919, the railway kept the north side of the city, which was home to the working class, away from the south side. The CP railway has always been

The mayor who never was: Nick at city council

the dividing line of Winnipeg, in terms of class politics and in terms of our history. Isabel Street had the only bridge and it was only two lanes; along with the Arlington Bridge those were the only two ways for North Enders to get downtown (and even then the Arlington really only gets you into the West End). Zuken wanted the bridge that would link the North End with the downtown so they could save driving, because as it stood, you would have to go all the way down Main Street to Portage before you would get downtown. That part made sense but he did not seem to realize what a solid and vibrant neighbourhood he was trying to expropriate. More than two hundred homes would have been destroyed if this had happened. Moving the underused railway yards would have not only avoided that whole problem, it would have solved many others.

CentreVenture, the city-created development corporation, has a mandate "to lead and encourage business investment and development downtown, and enhance the use of heritage buildings and land in the downtown area." While CentreVenture played a significant role in the development of Waterfront Drive and some other initiatives, Winnipeg needs to ask whether these projects have really revitalized the downtown in any significant way. I would say no. There is no way the downtown can be revitalized until its population rises from the current thirteen thousand to over fifty thousand. And that population needs to be diverse and secure. This doesn't come without significant direct investment. People are not going to move downtown just because there is an arena there. We also need a light railway transit system — a system where people leave their cars at home and take public transportation downtown in a clean and efficient manner. An electric, heritage streetcar system for the commercial core would also help.

Many questions remain unanswered. The old Metropolitan Theatre is finally being refurbished, but why has it sat empty and unused for so many years and what happened to the rock 'n' roll museum that was planned for the Met? When will we stop talking about a water park and actually build one? What happened to the thirty-eight-storey condominium tower at 100 Main Street? And what happened to all the other promised developments that have never occurred? Plan Winnipeg 2020 had lots of good ideas that have just faded away, not unlike the Plan Winnipeg 1993 document. Nick Ternette's Winnipeg wouldn't have allowed developers to scuttle true planning for their own gains.

The North Main Redevelopment Plan, under the leadership of Mary Richard and Joe Bova, was an initiative to revitalize the North Main area from Higgins to Portage. A Scottish village was planned, as well as an urban reserve. And what was the result? Thunderbird House and the Aboriginal Centre — that is really just about it! This was a great plan and it was ignored because that is an area where there aren't many voters and the people that do vote don't have money. If I had been mayor, that is not the way I would have made decisions! We had the opportunity, if not the obligation, to be leaders on the urban reserve issue and the city has not picked up the mantle. In 2003, the city produced a concise seventeen-page report, *First Steps: Municipal Aboriginal Pathways*, which is yet another document that set the foundation for vision, change and true development that was ignored by the powers that be.

When the Forks was first developed I saw it as an area for parks, recreation and museums. In 2000, I joined the Forks for People Not Profit, who argued for a green approach to the new development that would complement downtown rather than compete with it. Almost immediately, the city and Forks developers began to compromise the green space. Now, it's just cement and more cement. Stores and more stores. Had they followed up with our idea of the heritage streetcar, which would have been an attraction itself, the shopping core would be an enjoyable ride away and it could have been revived. Graham Avenue is a natural street to be a true pedestrian mall and the streetcar would have easily delivered people from the Forks to the shopping and vice versa. This would have maintained the integrity of the Forks as a place of peacefulness, education and recreation while allowing the streetcar to keep it connected to the arts community of the Exchange and the shopping on Portage and Graham.

We finally have the reality of Bus Rapid Transit (BRT) in Winnipeg as I write this early in 2012, but it is only a sliver of what is needed to transform Winnipeg from a city of two-car families to a city of zero-car families. I fear the current development is in the category of "too little, too late."

There is a rich fifty-year history of attempts to build a rapid transit system. Steve Juba, for those who remember our flamboyant 1960s mayor, is almost synonymous with the monorail he wanted to build and yet, the nearsightedness of council for the past fifty years means we have a few miles of pavement for buses and no clarity on what comes next or when. Imagine what our city would be like if a forceful initiative of light rail transit (LRT) using self-sustaining energy like they have in Calgary had been developed thirty-five years ago. The problems of urban sprawl and parking that plague our city would be greatly ameliorated. Developments would be geared to the railway and not to cars and be all the more attractive and efficient. People would feel completely different about coming downtown, and the presence of people would do more to deter crime and crime-related problems than any amount of policing can do.

As it is, the car culture of Winnipeg is so entrenched that small improvements to the present public transportation system (for example, heated bus shelters built with Plexiglas, air-conditioning in buses during the summer months and lower bus fares) is maybe all that most Winnipeggers want. We are talking about car ownership being up thirty percent in the past thirty years while transit use has dropped by an even greater percentage. Leadership in city hall is needed to change that comfort with the suburban car commute so that it is no longer the best option and so that LRT or moving downtown become the obvious choices. Only then will we truly turn around the inner city decay that is dealt with in the most superficial ways.

There are only two real issues facing our downtown. Housing and transportation! Without action on those, our downtown will continue to be the embarrassment that it is. Glen Murray was a great cheerleader for downtown and the Take Pride! slogan got us thinking, but it was never followed up with policy and development. In fact the Waverly West development went in the exact opposite direction. Low-density housing in an area where cars are a requirement was chosen over high-density housing in an area where public transit would be the obvious choice.

The Rapid Transit Task Force was created by city council in order to determine what kind of rapid transit options Winnipeg citizens would prefer. Well, that didn't happen. When they delivered their report in the fall of 2005, what was presented was a pre-determined option of what the task force considered to be a valid "rapid transit" system. As citizens, all that we were required to do was decide whether we agreed with that plan or not. Their proposal was merely a glorified express bus system. At least in 2000, the release of *Direction to the Future: The Guide to Better Transit in Winnipeg* was candid about the incredible decline in the use and quality of our bus system. Ultimately, it had little effect either. Buses remain a place for the poor in Winnipeg and, as long as it is kept that way, transit will be pushed down the agenda at city hall.

I remain in favour of anything that improves the present public transportation system because I am aware of many critics of our present transportation system that would like it privatized completely. However, I am vehemently opposed to any "con job" where the public is sold something that is called rapid transit when, in fact, it is not. To pass a BRT system as being the same as a LRT system is a sham! The 2005 report has become the status quo for Winnipeg in 2012.

Mayor Katz cancelled former mayor Glen Murray's BRT plan. The original recommendations of the task force were not to be dismissed on the way to the final report. That is, that the majority of those citizens involved in the consultation favoured some kind of rapid transit, either BRT or LRT (an LRT in the downtown area) and significant money for transit upgrades. Ultimately, the task force called for a significant increase in diamond lanes for buses, which Winnipeg Transit feels will create more traffic problems than they will alleviate. This is like using a slingshot to take down an elephant. Much bigger changes are needed to lead us out of our car culture.

Ultimately, the rising cost of gas will be the reason for some kind of rapid transit system in Winnipeg. The reality is that BRT technology has proven costly in the long run, inflexible and anything but rapid. All major cities have real LRT systems. Study after study proves that BRT attracts fewer riders and even fewer new riders than LRT. This nickel and diming is causing a slow bleed and nobody knows when the bleeding will stop. There were more transit vehicles on the road and more transit riders in 1986 than any year since, and our city has grown and driving has become more expensive. Something is wrong. Something is broken. Why is this happening in Winnipeg and not elsewhere? In some other cities, bus fares are increased, but ridership does not decrease. In Winnipeg, we have ghettoized public transportation. That is, for the majority of cases, only those who cannot afford a car take public transportation. In other cities, suburbanites leave their cars at home and take public transportation to work. Here, suburbanites prefer to buy a second car to solve their transportation problems. Even more frightening is just how ingrained the two-car culture is here. Even if bus fares were decreased, I fear that it would do little to increase bus ridership. Ridership will only increase when there is a significant improvement in the transit system, including service. People point to Ottawa's BRT system, where they have made significant efforts but the numbers do not show it as successful. It, too, is losing ridership and revenues and Ottawa is now seriously looking at converting it into an LRT system. If we want to talk about success, let's talk about the Calgary LRT system, which is completely wind-powered and is so successful that they are thinking of expanding it significantly with a current ridership of 250,000 people a day.

People who know me often comment on my consistency. My letters to the editor about every bus fare increase since it was raised from twenty-five cents back in the early seventies are just an example of what they point to. One issue that does challenge me to be so clear on is housing. I am a great proponent of rent controls to protect renters from abusive rent increases. Although property owners use condominium conversions and bogus renovations to get around these regulations, rent controls have their place in setting a standard. However, this is where my friends at the Frontier Centre for Public Policy and I have really disagreed. Their libertarian thinking says the market will meet the need for housing and they argue that rent controls have undermined the market and prevented developers from building for the inner core. I don't want to believe it but it is true that no affordable housing is being built by the private sector in the inner core. My solution would be to have massive investment in the kind of quality, subsidized housing that is the norm in Europe. Try looking for the slum area of Paris, France, some day. You are not going to find it. Look at the beautiful apartments and you'd be amazed to know they are full of subsidized tenants. I am convinced that all of these costs would be more than recouped with the savings in social services, corrections, medical care and all the other quality-of-life improvements that follow safe, secure, affordable housing to build a life upon. There is currently a "housing first" study going on in Winnipeg and unless it is tripped up by political interference it will surely show this is an investment in people that goes a long way and that an ounce of prevention is worth a pound of cure.

We all know Winnipeg as a city of neighbourhoods. People often identify themselves by the neighbourhood they live in. This is exactly the kind of parochialism that Unicity sought to end. There is much to say about the legacy of Unicity and a speech of mine on this topic is available on the website of the Frontier Centre for Public Policy. Amalgamation is a dual-edged sword because the identity that prevents us from big-city thinking creates wonderful neighbourhoods. Unfortunately, a lynchpin of our communities — our community clubs — was sacrificed in the changes that came with Unicity. We had decentralized recreational programs in the 1950s and the 1960s, all the way up to 1975. Every community centre had a program director and a janitor, paid for by the city through the Department of Recreation. They were responsible to work with the volunteers and the board of directors of each community centre to establish programming. In 1975, city council tore out that whole program and centralized recreation. They created these consultants and told community centres to raise their own money and hire their own staff. The suburbs were rich enough to afford to hire professional people to run programming and they still do that. The inner-city clubs can't raise the money to do that and they have suffered greatly. It is like a Darwinian "survival of the fittest" approach to our very recreation of community and selves. With all the advancement of gambling by the government, including bingo halls, casinos and the ever-present video-lotto terminals, the local bingos that supported the inner-city clubs died out. Community centres, especially in the poorer parts of the city, just went downhill. Some recreation staff came to me and told me privately that they agree with me. The change to the community centre structure was carried out with little consultation and intimidation that prevented the common sense feedback that might have changed the process. If you staff the community centre, you can make it work; if you don't have staff, you can't.

This is at the core of what it means to be a Winnipegger: Winnipeggers participate in their communities! Programs have now become something for the wealthy and elite. Look at where the recreational programs are available in the Leisure Guide. The city pays lip service to the need for programs to keep kids off the streets, while Mayor Sam Katz makes his backroom deals with wealthy organizations like Teens for Christ to build mega-centres of dubious community value without public consultation. Yet, we let the institutions right in the middle of our neighbourhoods dry up right before our eyes. In the past, sports, which are probably the best way to keep young people focused and healthy, were supported by the common purse of the community. Now, the parents who can afford it write big cheques for their kids. For those who cannot afford it, there are very few sports outside of soccer that are cheap to play.

Is there a lesson to be learned from closing these smaller community centres in favour of developing huge, mega-community centres? My suspicion is that the decline and ultimate death of community centres in the inner city began back in 1975 and the changes have been so insidious that it will be hard to demonstrate the impact of the closure of any one particular centre.

I remember being a coach and a volunteer (vice-president of the West End Community Centre — now called the Burton Cummings Community Centre) in the 1960s. Back then, community centres were the hub of recreation and leisure activities. Everyone congregated at the community centres, including families and kids on sports teams. Everyone walked to his or her local community centre. No one took a car, as is common today. In fact, I can remember chaperoning Friday night teen dances, featuring Chad Allan and the Expressions (who eventually evolved into the Guess Who), where more than four hundred kids packed the community centre! And, believe me, every community centre had bands playing on weekends. (The Squires, Neil Young's band, and The Devrons, Burton Cummings' first band, were also popular.) Kids packed the centres because there wasn't much else to do.

Even more importantly, community centres were decentralized whether they were big or small. The program director, in conjunction with the board of directors (volunteers), developed programs for that particular community centre. Different centres had different programs depending on the needs of the particular community. The significance of a paid program director was that the person was trained to develop recreational programming. He or she would work with the board of directors to determine what programs were best for that particular community centre and determine who was needed to make those programs successful. On the one level, volunteers were recruited to coach group sports, such as hockey, baseball, football and soccer. In other cases, if the community clubs were too small, program directors would arrange for schools to remain open so that classes like yoga and gymnastics could be taught by professionals hired by the city. I know we live in a changing world, but creative solutions such as tax credits or other incentives for volunteers were never even tried.

Admittedly, there is another factor in the decline of community centres in the inner city. Today there are endless choices for recreation and leisure activities in our lives — quite different from the 1960s and 1970s: twenty-four-hour sports on television, movies, video games and the Internet, to name a few. People are more sedentary and less likely to be involved in activities outside their homes. Now, when the city builds its new mega-centres, offering lots of programming and lots of free parking, they will most likely be located primarily in suburban communities where there is adequate space for parking, as opposed to the inner city where there is little parking available. This will lead to a further decline of community centres in the inner city.

Solutions are possible! One of the possible solutions to the continued closure of inner city community centres would be to give community associations the option to buy community centre facilities from the city for $1 and run their own programs independently from the City of Winnipeg Recreation and Leisure Services Department. Instead of having padlocked, rundown centres open to vandalism, communities would be able to attract federal and provincial grants as a non-profit group and run neighbourhood centres with a variety of different programs, which would result in less crime and would keep people engaged in their community.

The City of Winnipeg's Recreation and Leisure budget under the Community Services Department has been on a serious downhill slide for the past twenty or twenty-five years. It is ridiculous and I have been saying this ever since it began in 1975. It takes more than a seventy-five dollar federal tax credit. Running recreation programs in a city like Winnipeg takes real investment in equipment and in people working in the community who can stay with the kids to keep them involved. The split we have between the inner city and the suburbs in terms of these sports just never had to happen.

People have talked about a water park for years. Given our long cold winters, it makes some sense. However, it is a lie to say that it could define a community. The thinking that it will only come with private-public partnership is also flawed. When this happens, taxpayers end up subsidizing private entrepreneurs and wind up with no control over these ventures. It is the worst of both worlds. Put simply, investing in supporting communities should mean investing in communities and developing the neighbourhoods of all Winnipeggers of all incomes.

As I suggested, we have somehow managed to both undermine the true organic communities in our city while at the same time allowing the "not in my back yard" thinking that remains part of our city ethos. The mayor and Executive Policy Committee have a very clear sense of direction, which is that the city ought to be run like a business. All policies that they develop relate to that direction. I can envision significant difficulty for any co-ordination of different voices to be heard at city hall. Even though they might agree on issues related to a fundamental topic like recreation, Liberal-left coalitions do not work in this city. Winnipeg politics are split between the inner city and suburbia, with Wolseley and Fort Rouge/Lord Roberts being the only exceptions. Council has to see beyond their traditional alliances in order to run a city like a city instead of like a business. This applies to almost any major issue you can name.

Unicity ensured the marginalization of the NDP at city hall. It was only after 1987 that the municipal wing of the NDP decided, for practical reasons, to get out of civic politics and a new organization, Winnipeg Into the '90s (WIN), was born. This body attempted to transcend traditional NDP support by bringing progressive Liberals into a new coalition. Unfortunately, the mixture of different ideologies failed to gel.

In the 1970s, the NDP government decided it was time Winnipeg grew up. It was time to end the "small towns" of Winnipeg — St. James, St. Boniface and nine more, each of which had its own city council — and create one big city, namely Winnipeg. While Sidney Green put forth that Unicity was created for tax purposes only, that is, the provincial government wanted Winnipeg's downtown to stop subsidizing the suburbs (meaning that the suburbanites benefit from the downtown infrastructure without paying for it with taxes), it also had an ideological basis: others in Schreyer's NDP government saw parochialism as a problem in and of itself, and started looking at the city as a whole. That meant the amalgamation of twelve more or less small municipalities into one city, with an elected city council whose fifty members would elect the mayor and set citywide policies to be implemented by community committees. This is not what happened. Mayor Stephen Juba persuaded Premier Schreyer to allow the mayor's position to be elected citywide and while the city council did set citywide policies it also, unsuccessfully, tried to administer them at the same time.

Well, the Unicity plan did not work as it was envisioned: city council today is rife with parochialism, just as it was forty years ago. We need look no further than St. Norbert Councillor Justin Swandel's comments in an August 19, 2008, letter to the editor of the *Winnipeg Free Press* on banning pesticides and establishing a police commission: "I have not received a single phone call concerning a ban on pesticides and the establishment of a police commission," he said. "So why should I vote for it?" I've always felt that councillors are not only parochial, but they are typical of the division between the inner city and the suburbs I have been talking about. But it's more than that. The fact is, Winnipeg is not a city at all. It is a grouping of twenty-nine (or more) distinct neighbourhoods that make up a large town.

I know, for example, people who live in St. James who have never gone downtown or, for that matter, to any other community in Winnipeg. They were born in, they live in and will die in St. James. I have discovered that, outside of a few regional spots that do attract people from all over Winnipeg (Assiniboine Park, The Forks, Rainbow Stage) you will not find people who live in one area using recreation centres, malls and so on in another area. They stay within their own neighbourhood. Cities like Toronto and Vancouver have distinct neighbourhoods, but they have something that Winnipeg lacks: an urban culture. A lot of Winnipeggers (with the exception of immigrants and Aboriginal people) come from farming communities. Consequently, they bring with them a rural mindset that contributes to Winnipeg's small-town atmosphere. Former mayor Glen Murray (probably the only mayor who had a citywide vision) brought in Richard Florida, author of a very popular trilogy, *The Rise of the Creative Class*, *Cities of the Creative Class* and *The Flight of the Creative Class*, to talk about what a city could be. Florida created indexes that rate cities by a "Bohemian Index," a "Gay Index," a "Diversity Index" and similar criteria and suggests that true urban development comes from who is there, not what is there. Social infrastructure is more important than physical infrastructure. People don't move to where jobs are but jobs move to where people are!

You don't have to buy into Florida's ideas completely to accept that he is reminding us that this is the twenty-first century. Murray's attempt to convince citizens of Winnipeg's potential, however, was lost. The audience was overwhelmed by Florida's ideas. Why? We couldn't get past our Prairie small-town thinking to look towards creating an urban culture. Small towns are dying out. It's time to grow up. Winnipeg must develop an urban culture — that is, as Richard Florida suggests, a creative class of artists, architects and entrepreneurs who work together and have a vision of the city as a whole. We could then envelop the uniqueness of neighbourhoods, then transcend those neighbourhoods into a citywide urban culture that would allow Winnipeg to contend with other large cities like Toronto and Vancouver and move into the twenty-first century. He sums up his ideas with what he calls the four Ts: technology, talent, tolerance (diversity) and territorial assets (the things that are real and authentic about the city). Unfortunately, I don't see any history or even much anticipation that this creative thinking will be at the heart of our city council's leadership.

Even though he disappointed me in many ways, Glen Murray was the best mayor in the last fifty years. He had a clear vision of what Winnipeg could be and attempted to transform the way Winnipeg finances itself. He had a rare combination of outstanding intellect and captivating charisma. He could connect with anyone and when asked would remind others that he was "the first Labour-endorsed mayor of Winnipeg since John Queen in the 1930s."

I guess time softens my views. When he left I was essentially glad to see him go but even as soon as September 2006 when he returned to the city and I had a chance to hear him speak I saw a man of dreams and a man of vision who I still think could have been more than he was for our city. One of the many ideas that Murray pursued but did not succeed in delivering was the incorporation of the "Indianapolis Bidding Model," developed in the 1990s. At the heart of this vision, for me, was the opportunity for civic employees to compete with private industry for city contracts. With union endorsement and cooperation, this approach can be a very effective way of completing the important work that a city has to take on. The Frontier Centre for Public Policy brought Nick Newton here from England to talk about how this system revived and renewed London's bus system, the biggest in the world. They also brought Steve Fantauzzo, a union leader from

Indianapolis, to talk about the successes of their work in delivering services to the community in a fiscally responsible way. A key component in the program is that the bids were evaluated not on profit as a bottom line but on meeting public need. In Indianapolis, unions were winning over eighty percent of the contracts and were able to institute profit-sharing programs for their membership. Public unions and businesses compete to provide the best service to that end and provide tax saving that Winnipeggers could barely even imagine.

The final dream I would entertain in the "What if I Were Mayor?" scenario is that I would have continually sought the provincial/municipal cooperation to implement a guaranteed annual income system. Such a system is a key way to rid ourselves of a welfare system that leaves people in poverty while diminishing their self-esteem and belief in opportunity and wasting all sorts of resources in the duplication and monitoring of services. The guaranteed annual income approach is highly efficient in delivering income security that allows people more dignity than any system that has existed in my lifetime. It recognizes that many people are better off being free to do the real work of caring for family members, volunteering in important work that is not seen as worthy for pay and tending to their own needs of health and wellness. Not a replacement for capitalism, it is a holistic approach that accounts for life beyond profit. Sadly, it has simply never gathered the political will to move ahead and yet it could change our cities and our country for the better in recognition that truly cooperative community has no trouble living by the dictum, "from each according to ability, to each according to need." There was a great opportunity in 2002 when Louise Gosselin, a Montreal welfare recipient, asked the Supreme Court to grant the right to "a guaranteed standard of living" in her *Charter* complaint that "workfare" programs violated the *Charter of Rights and Freedoms*. Unfortunately, the court ruled five to four against her. Had one of the justices voted the other way, the door might have been opened for a national guaranteed annual income strategy.

8

My Exile

"If you want to make a living here, if you want to survive in this country, you stay quiet, you don't talk, you don't write letters."

S ometimes even strangers ask me if I've ever had a real job. I have had many, but given my reputation and my commitments, my work life has been storied and "uneven," to say the least. In the late 1970s, I was applying all over Canada for jobs and, unexpectedly, I heard from Frontier College. Frontier College is an adult education centre out of Toronto, which was known in the 1950s and 1960s for teaching English as a second language to newcomers. I recognized the name because my father had taken courses with them. They sent teachers to northern communities and taught people, often immigrant workers, English. They were also doing some community development work, which I didn't even know they were involved in. They asked me to work for them in Christopher Lake, in northern Saskatchewan. I couldn't even begin to find Christopher Lake on a map, but I needed a job and they were offering me one. Next thing I knew I was in Toronto for training, which was solid and even included Saul Alinsky's ideas. The whole project was a little vague though; they told me I would "work with the local Métis association," but by the time I got there, I discovered there was no Métis association. There was one person who pretended he was an organization and he didn't do anything.

Being a white person working in an Aboriginal community was a challenge in the first place and I felt like I was in exile. Secondly, in small towns of a few hundred people, outsiders are seen as outsiders and often as agitators or, if the mood is right, as communists! I lasted six and a half months, and I did work that I thought was just. I tried to expose the racism in the community and the Saskatoon *Star-Phoenix* published a big story about my naming the unspoken racism, but I was isolated completely. There was no one with whom to share a victory and no one to soothe the bruises. There were not even people to just sit and talk with. Everyone met me with suspicion. My family came out there for a while, but it was hell. The housing was completely inadequate. My daughter, her mother and I lived in a small hunting shack with no drinking water and it was cold. This doesn't mean it wasn't interesting and I don't have some fond memories. I certainly don't regret going there. It was, as they say, "a learning experience." I had spoken out against a condominium development and those who stood to benefit from it had connections. My presence at the local town hall meeting and the coverage in the Saskatoon paper was more opposition than they were accustomed to. When I say I left after six and a half months, it is more accurate to say that I was, literally, physically kicked out of that community. The RCMP came to get me but I told them, "I'll leave when I leave."

I could only stand feeling useless for so long, so I asked Frontier College to send me to another place, which ended up being Eagle River in northwest Ontario. That was a little better, because they wanted to set up a drop-in centre for the kids, and I actually did accomplish something. We got a drop-in centre started and it still functions today. I lived with a family during the week. On weekends, I would go back to Winnipeg. I came to know people who were doing great things in the Aboriginal community. It was a good pick-me-up after the Christopher Lake experience.

My next job was as program director at the Indian-Métis Friendship Centre in Sioux Lookout, Ontario. I was interviewed, and I wound up sleeping outside because the hotel rooms were booked and I couldn't find anywhere to stay. Nevertheless, I got the job. Only later did I discover that I got the job because there were four whites and three Aboriginals on the board. All the whites voted for me, and all Aboriginals voted against me. Sioux Lookout, like all of these towns I worked in, was racist beyond belief. There was a complete division: Aboriginals on one side, and whites on the other, with no interaction between them. It was just an awful environment. The politics were vicious. In spite of the craziness around me, I did a lot of work there, because it was a Friendship Centre and it was set up for programming. I brought in folk singer Fred Penner and other performers and I did all kinds of small stuff such as writing for the community paper. I kept busy and felt I contributed. My daughter and her mother also came to live with me here. Again, we were in a house that was falling apart. It was a rough situation, but I liked the work. I liked the kids: we established regular ping-pong tournaments, we had dart tournaments, we wound up organizing all kinds of programs and the place was packed with youth all the time. The teens were oblivious to all the politics and that worked for me. The Centre was open from ten in the morning until ten at night and I was there seven days a week. I never took a holiday, not even a weekend break. It was crazy. I could not have done it for much longer even though there was a lot to like.

I had lived in cities (Berlin and Winnipeg) all my life and I wasn't really made for a life where things were always expected to be "the way they always were before." I was at my wit's end not knowing what to do. I couldn't buy a job. I went to what was called the Unemployment Insurance Commission at the time and I had a counsellor assigned to me to make sure my résumé was up to date and that I was ready to look for work. His job actually included finding opportunities. I can't remember his name but he was a very nice guy. He knew who I was and had helped me before. In six months, he sent me to two interviews. He said, "I have sent out your résumé, which is an excellent résumé, to 110 places in Winnipeg." Of that, only two people would interview me. The common answer was, "Ternette? The communist? We won't touch him with a ten-foot pole! There is no way we will ever interview him. How dare you send his résumé to us?" My employment counsellor was completely honest with me. There was nobody who was going to hire me in Winnipeg. Everyone was scared of me. After striking out in the three Aboriginal communities, I looked at Calgary as a place to start anew. When I was offered a job interview in Calgary, I was keen to go.

I've been on unemployment insurance nine or ten times, and have taken food from food banks where I volunteered, but I have never applied for actual welfare. It is my mother's voice that I can still hear: "Never go on welfare, never!" People laugh at me because I've worked with lots of welfare recipients and many I consider as friends. I have fought for people to get welfare and to make welfare more user-friendly for people who need it. There is obviously nothing morally wrong with accepting help, but not needing welfare is the only expectation my parents ever put on me. So I can say, "At least I've fulfilled my mother's request, I've never been on welfare." I've been in pretty harsh situations. One thing that I know is there's no such thing as freedom of speech in this country. It's there, but you pay a price. If you're not prepared to pay a price, forget it. If you want to make a living here, if you want to survive in this country, you stay quiet, you don't talk, you don't write letters.

You have to understand, I was writing hundreds of letters, mostly to newspapers. I started writing letters in 1970. I've had twelve hundred letters published in my lifetime. I still write letters. I became a professional letter-writer, that's what some people call me, which I don't mind. People called me a nuisance because I got involved in any controversial issue, and I got lots of media coverage. In the 1970s activism was big and the media liked covering activists, but not these days. Then, you were part of "a generation." Now, you are just a wacko. Is there anyone filling that role in Winnipeg now? Is there an activist so popular and engaged that he or she is regularly mistaken for an elected politician? I don't see anyone like that. This is what ran me out of town and it is why I went to court to try to ensure others were protected from such discrimination.

People often ask me if I liked my time in Calgary, and they are usually quite surprised when I tell them how much I did. In many ways, the city is a polar opposite to Winnipeg. Even in the 1980s, it was a very Americanized city. Money counted. Ethnicity didn't and it still doesn't. If Calgary has ethnic neighbourhoods, they are hard to find. Chinatown was about the only kind of visible neighbourhood I encountered and this was quite a change from the city of neighbourhoods that is Winnipeg. Very few Aboriginals live in Calgary. I worked on reserves outside Calgary and as long as they had money when they came to town, there wasn't the kind of racism that exists in Winnipeg. In Calgary, the only colours that mattered were the colours on the bills people spent. Most of the money, including that coming from reserves that are relatively well off, connects to the oil business. I did what I had to do to fit in. I wore a cowboy hat when I had to, like during the Stampede. Being a Russian German was never an issue there the way it mattered in Winnipeg. I was just as visible there in the media. I was on community TV, I wrote for the newspapers and I ran for city council in 1983. I was the only socialist to run for city council, and I only got 25 votes but the media loved me. I was like a new toy. A socialist in Calgary civic politics was a true novelty and I played up on it. I often satirized the mainstream media and had fun with it.

Although I was there about five years, I didn't make many friends. I lived in an inner-city neighbourhood, Hillhurst Sunnyside, which was a lot like Wolseley in Winnipeg in terms of the age of the houses and the congregation of more liberal-minded people. My job took me into the inner city in the not-for-profit housing sector. At the time, Calgary was significantly ahead of what was going on in social housing programs in Winnipeg. I worked with Peter Globensky for much of my time there and we were tireless. We worked on discrete and constructive projects that we had great success with, such as building and managing non-for-profit housing units. We also worked on much less tangible projects like helping the neighbourhood organize against the expropriations to make way for the LRT system. While we were able to get some concessions to the grade on 10th and 9A Streets, and helped organize people to ask for a fair expropriation price, we were not successful in securing the major changes we were seeking. Elaine Husband was city councillor (1983–1989) for the area, and she worked quite closely with us. She remains an assiduous worker for her community. Gerhard Gross, who had trained with Saul Alinsky, was also on staff and we worked morning, noon and night in order to meet the people where they were, rather than expecting them to come to us. Birgit Becker was the receptionist who did very well to work with the three of us who were all high-energy people. Peter will still talk about our lunches. We often ate at the same Chinese place on 10th Street, where at the end of the meal he would pretend to pick the food off his shirt that he said that I spat at him when I was talking with my mouth full and then proceed to direct me to my own beard, where other escaped morsels rested.

On the environmental front, there was a lot to like as well. Even then, Calgary had bicycle paths all over the city. They did not dare use malathion for mosquitoes. They saw it for what it was: a cancer-causing agent. Even Ralph Klein banned it in 1982. As mayor, he banned all sorts of carcinogens and ran a more health-conscious city then than Winnipeg is now. They were doing a lot of things right. They built the LRT in the early eighties, right when I moved there. I saw how it changed the attitudes of people, how people got out of their cars. There were half as many cars in the downtown by 1985 as there are in Winnipeg today! It is a bigger city with a lot more money and you would expect the opposite. Since 2001, wind-powered electricity runs the public train transportation system in Calgary. I get embarrassed when I start comparing. Do we refuse to do this in Winnipeg just so we don't lose any jobs at local bus manufacturer, Flyer Industries? I've never yet been given a decent explanation as to why we can't do what they have done.

I came to know Ralph Klein. I used to have drinks with him. I guess a lot of people did. He liked to drink and it was getting the better of him but he would come to the downtown and we would have a drink and talk about politics. This is when he was a mayor, not when he became premier. I always enjoyed my time with him. He was passionate about Aboriginal issues and really wanted to hear from me about what I knew was going on in the community. I wouldn't call us close, and we did not have the kind of ideological discussions I have with others. It was more that he was a good politician, listening to and finding out about his city. Publicly, he was a very good storyteller, maybe he was pumping me for stories to share so others could see he was in touch with his constituents.

I got involved in demonstrations in Calgary too. I helped organize May Day. The left there was much smaller than in Winnipeg. There were a few communists around, and I met them quickly and I came to know a few anarchists but there were not a lot of people for me to work with. The media never became tired of the idea of a socialist moving to Calgary to find work. They had as much fun with that my last year as they did my first. I even came close to settling in for the long haul but I experienced something Winnipeg never has. There was a boom-bust in the 1980s. It was what we called "the oil crisis" when oil and gas prices shot up to record highs. When I was there, there was two billion dollars' worth of construction going on in 1980 and then by 1982 there was less than a hundred million dollars' worth of construction going on. Winnipeg never sees that kind of swing and everywhere in Calgary there were empty and unfinished buildings. People just walked off the jobs to make sure they got their last paycheck, knowing they could not cover their mortgage. I saw people walking out of $150,000–$200,000 homes. Today, these same homes are worth $700,000 or more. There was significant unemployment too. When I first came to Calgary, there was a job for everyone, but by 1983, there was about an eleven percent unemployment rate. I left in 1985 and it didn't get better until about 1986 when the oil situation started to improve and the Winter Olympics gave a boost to the economy. This all influenced my thinking, in terms of urban development, because all that activity prevented leaders from having vision. When things started to shut down, a lot of personal depression followed and the suicide rate jumped. I lost friends to suicide and I am sure most people who lived there at the time have a similar story to tell. The economy doesn't have the same impact in Winnipeg. It was very hard for me to put what was going on into context, to understand the idea that people would take their own lives due to a downturn in the economy. In Winnipeg, the downturns are less drastic and we just roll with it.

My partner, Bev, and our daughter, Tegan, came with me to Calgary but moved to Montreal before I left the city. I lived in a number of small apartments and rooming houses. They were all adequate. In one, I converted the living room into a library by bringing in a stack of old crates and placing them in rows to keep all my books. My friend Peter Globensky liked to come over to peruse and borrow books.

It was a difficult time for me in personal ways as my daughter and her mother stopped living with me. My parents were aging. I wasn't around the Winnipeg friends that I had been close to for years. I met many interesting people in Calgary but I wouldn't call them friends. One of the ways I met people was through community TV. One person I remember is Lance Regan, who billed himself as a "Trance Medium." He came on my show and went into a trance and then spoke from it. One reporter made a comment about what great TV it was to watch me listen to a guy talking in his sleep. Lance had a degree in engineering and walked away from it to follow what he saw as a calling. The single life, which applied to me, I guess, was popular and I interviewed various people who were on the cutting edge of introduction services and dating clubs. People didn't consider themselves "above" community TV in any way and newspaper editors, elected officials, professors and others were all quite happy to be my guests, and these people were all brand new to me. But just because I had access to all these people didn't mean I stopped having edgier guests on my show. I never hesitated to bring marginalized people, such as sex trade workers, on my show either.

My five years in Calgary also helped me appreciate the arts community in Winnipeg more than I had before. I was always a member of the Royal Winnipeg Ballet and the Winnipeg Symphony Orchestra and always saw whichever show I could afford, but I took them for granted. Calgary didn't even come close in comparison. They had some good avant-garde theatre and some young people doing art that pushed the edges, but they had nothing like Winnipeg has. In my view, this connects to Calgary's lack of ethnic and racial diversity and its lack of history. It is as if you get stamped "Calgarian" when you arrive and your history is unimportant, although that can change in a hurry when the economy is bad. Ralph Klein actually called the Newfoundlanders "foreigners" and told them to go home when work became scarce in Alberta.

On the historical front, in Calgary it often seems as if there is a by-law that any building more than ten years old has to be torn down. There hasn't been and still isn't anything in place to prevent the destruction of their history. It just is not part of their mindset. People generally don't "stick it out" there and, with the mayor telling people to leave, it is not surprising. If you don't have money you can't stay there, so you move on. This is so different from Winnipeg, where it is simply home to people and when you suffer through unemployment, it never occurs to you to move on. It makes for a very different fabric and I was part of that fabric. For my entire time in Calgary I was working on short-term contracts and, although I was doing okay, I was one missed paycheck away from being homeless. The economy seemed to be getting worse, so when my father got sick and he called to say, "Come home," I did. I moved back and took care of him for the last five years of his life. I lived with him and helped him out. If the right job had come, I might have stayed, but at that time, I was better off being poor in Winnipeg than getting by in Calgary.

The biggest event for me over those years was the death of my mother in 1983. It was hard being away and I had to ask my dear friend, Willie Sheard, to ensure she followed up with my mother's medical care. As I said earlier, she didn't even want palliative care, thinking it was God's will that she suffer. It was difficult when she died because she wanted to be cremated, which the Russian Orthodox Church of the Holy Trinity on Manitoba Avenue did not support. Her service to the church was recognized because they had a Metropolitan, Valdimir Nagosky, officiate, but because of her insistence on being cremated, they only provided the evening vesper service and a shortened liturgy the day of the burial. My father died eight years later, in March 1990, fifteen years after retiring from the municipal hospitals. My church's priest refused my father last communion and last rites, and did not even attend, let alone lead, his memorial service, saying, "Your father was not devout." This arrogant and judgmental priest did certainly not help me adjust to the idea that the only two relatives I ever had real contact with, my mother and father, were gone.

9

The Media

"I will debate and talk on television, radio and in newspapers anytime and anywhere."

When my picture appeared in the *Winnipeg Free Press* after I was arrested at the Festival Express concert in 1970, I was pretty much a hardline Marxist. I had rejected the media as being little more than a tool of the rich. We thought that the media was bourgeois. Shortly thereafter, even though I had graduated, I began writing for *The Uniter*, the University of Winnipeg student newspaper. I also took part in frequent debates with libertarians there on various issues. Getting at those ideas was what drove my interest in newspaper writing. But it was the same media that I wrote for that labelled me an anti-Canadian communist and took every opportunity they could to trash me. Yet, I realized that you simply could not avoid the media. I couldn't beat them, so I joined them.

Bill Harnum was the editor at *The Uniter*, and he was a serious libertarian. A number of us on the left opposed to his ideas did what we could, including petitioning, to have him removed because he treated the paper as a business and saw himself as a dictator rather than a democratic leader. I liked him personally — we enjoyed talking politics — I just deplored the Ayn Rand-type ideas he espoused and published. Ironically, after he left the paper under pressure, the governing board got rid of me too.

Winnipeg was quite a hotbed for libertarianism in the sixties and seventies. Leonard Peikoff, one of the truly big names in the movement, is from Winnipeg. He and others moved to be with Ayn Rand in New York. *The Passion of Ayn Rand* was written by Barbara Brandon, a Winnipegger whose husband Nathaniel Brandon had an affair with Rand. Ray Torgrud was another follower. His wife was libertarian too. Clancy Smith, the head of the Libertarian Party of Canada, was another Winnipegger connected to the big names of the movement in New York.

It is not as if there isn't some agreement between myself and the libertarians. Rand opposed the Vietnam War before the left did. Ron Paul, who ran for U.S. president in 2012, is a libertarian from Texas who opposes all wars and calls America an imperialist nation. There are great stories about debates in the 1940s between Roland Penner and Barbara Brand and other debates between socialists and libertarians. We've got lots to talk about. Israel Asper, known then as Izzy, became the leader of the Manitoba Liberals with an eye to convert them into a libertarian party. We used to have coffee regularly because the Liberal and NDP offices were both near the Maryland Bridge, and I was around there a lot. Israel was very informal, very approachable and he loved to talk politics. He always made time for me. Although there is no formal party with a libertarian agenda in Manitoba, the strong tradition of thinking is still reflected in many ways, perhaps most publicly through the Frontier Centre for Public Policy, where my friend Peter Holle is president.

In many ways, it was that libertarian community that motivated me to write. After writing for *The Uniter*, I became a regular writer of letters to the editor to the papers in Winnipeg, and I am still known as much for that as for anything. A little later, in 1973, I started listening to CBC and I noticed they would take people who had opinions and give them two minutes to say what they had to say, so I started writing opinion pieces and sent them into CBC and they liked it! I wound up being on radio in the morning, with Lesley Hughes. That's how I met Lesley Hughes, doing broadcasts of opinion pieces on civic and other issues. I also met another lifelong friend, Ross Dobson, through this work. They were committed to staying away from PPPS ("permanent program personalities") and wanted diversity of character and viewpoint, so I was perfect for them. It was core stuff, like what it meant to me to identify myself as a leftist. They paid fifty dollars for me to tell the city what I thought about things.

Then, I started writing columns for the *Winnipeg Free Press*. The more I was "out there," the more vocal those who opposed me became. One who consistently trashed me was Shaun Herron, who later carved a very successful career as a novelist. He had a little column called "The Herron Folk," and I often made it in there. I never once met him face to face. Not long after I started with the *Winnipeg Free Press*, and as my name became more recognizable, the *Winnipeg Tribune* asked me to write columns. They didn't pay me, but they let me do features and I began to develop a following. I worked regularly for the *Tribune* up until few years before they stopped publishing in 1980. Ray Torgrud asked me to appear on his CJAY-TV show, as they used to have editorial comments on their news broadcast, and they would pay me for my appearances. I even learned how to use the teleprompter. Maybe I could have become a sports reporter, even with my accent. Maybe the National Broadcasting School didn't know what they were talking about when they told me to "lose my accent" when I was a teenager. I was on radio and TV many, many times in the 1970s.

I also had a show on CJUM, the radio station at the University of Manitoba. I covered the gamut with that one with specials where I played records of the Belgian singer Jacques Brel, the pioneering Kingston Trio, East German balladeer Wolf Bierman and other musicians who bridged the gap between social commentary and entertainment, including my favourite, Phil Ochs.

The paying work dried up in the early 1980s, but I would still get published by the university papers, *The Manitoban* and *The Uniter*. I liked getting my ideas out. When I went to Calgary, the *Calgary Herald* and the *Calgary Sun* published columns I wrote. My voice was unique out there. The *Calgary Sun*, as you would expect, was a right-wing rag, and they didn't pay me. I found out they paid their other writers and when I demanded payment, they cut off all their guest columnists from the community. Both Calgary papers, however, printed many of my letters to the editor. I also met the community TV people shortly after I arrived in Calgary and was on the air within six months.

When I came back to Winnipeg, I was writing a little for the *Winnipeg Sun*, but they were also publishing as many as three or more of my letters each week. They were locally owned at that point and were truly trying to serve the community. I was happy they were so welcoming, even though my letters were followed by snide little editorial responses. I competed for a job being their "token left-wing columnist," but Doug Smith beat me out. He had his credentials and he did a good job. He has gone on to write and publish several books but is probably best known for a very good biography of Joe Zuken.

From 1987 to about 1991 I was a regular contributor to 1290 Talk Radio, which was in competition against Peter Warren on CJOB. Of course, they never even come close. They wanted me as a civic reporter. I was to work with Gerald Fast and others, such as ultra-right-winger John Colson. When the format of 1290 changed, Gerald changed his career by going to Advance Electronics, where he did quite well for himself. This was the most right-wing station you could imagine, but they were constantly interviewing me. I had the opportunity to talk about all the civic issues. Susan Thompson was mayor and there was no shortage of stuff to disagree with her about. I enjoyed it even if it didn't pay.

Uptown, then an independent community newspaper, hired me in 1999. I had done some freelance with them in the past but they hired me as a regular columnist. For seven years, I wrote every week at thirty-five dollars a pop. I wrote well over three hundred columns for them. Then they took me off, because I was too old, they said. This was after *Uptown* was bought by the *Winnipeg Free Press* and they were up front that they were after the twenty-five to thirty-four demographic, and I understood that.

I enjoy writing. These days, I send stuff to both the *Free Press* and the *Sun*. If they publish it, they publish it, and if they don't, they don't. I get paid sometimes. Other times, I don't.

I've only said no to the media once since 1970, when my daughter's partner got into legal trouble for presenting himself as a lawyer when he wasn't a lawyer, and somebody in the media discovered that he was with my daughter and they wanted to come to my home and interview me about this. I absolutely refused! I said I will not talk about my daughter or any other family member. That's the only time I've ever said no to the media, because I wasn't going to drag my family into anything. Their story would grow legs if my name was attached. It would have been very unfair to them. But outside of that, since 1970, I have been interviewed hundreds, maybe thousands of times on network television, commercial radio and community television and radio.

I did my own television show for twenty years, from 1972 to 1992. I met scads of interesting people (including my wife!). I got to work with some real visionaries, like Syd Boyling, who ran Videon, the cable company, and really believed in the community component. Dorothy Dunsmore, who managed the station at its very beginning, was also a woman of vision, conviction and talent. It was a privilege to work with her and so many others. Donna Johnson handled all the booking and did a great job bringing a spirit of generosity to everything she did. I enjoyed my time there, not only because of the unique platform, but because of the culture of the station.

Unlike other cities where community cable stations provided access to only a small part of the city, Videon, although licensed to broadcast only in the west side of the city, would broadcast the community shows throughout the city. In the early days, anyone who wanted to was given access and the studio ran from early in the morning until late at night seven days a week. Ironically, as they improved the technical aspects and became more professional looking, they became less welcoming of the community and, by the mid-nineties, it was nothing like it had been in its inception. What Shaw Television does now bears no resemblance to the true community access station that I worked at. Several people ran their shows for years. There were shows for the Filipino community, the Dutch community, seniors, Girl Guides and more. Some shows were dedicated to local music but the most common topic was religion; there was no end to those who wanted to get on their soapbox. Perhaps the one show that stands out in particular was *Coming Out*, primarily the work of Chris Vogel, who might rightly be called "Manitoba's first gay activist." It was a true honour to have worked with such a brave man, who ran his show from 1980 to 1994. As an activist who sought the right to marry another man in 1974, he was ahead of his time. I am sure he is thankful for the fruits of his many years at the forefront when many of his supporters were unable or unwilling to identify themselves. He tells a story of a man who bought one of those miniature three- or four-inch televisions and hid it inside his own house so his family would not know he was watching the show.

One incarnation of my show was under the name *Crossfire*, which I did with a right-leaning insurance advisor named Laurie Fischer. Laurie was the "calm, unassuming" half and I was the "feisty, fulminating" half of the team and we discussed all sorts of topics from insurance choices to seeking peace in Palestine. Martin Boroditsky, former radio announcer, and a few others, also played "the other half" on my show.

The particular episode of my twenty years in television that I recall most fondly is when Robert Steen granted me an hour-long interview, the first one, when he was elected mayor. I also did shows with Bud Sherman, a former broadcaster who became a cabinet minister, my former professor Lloyd Axworthy and Ed Schreyer, whom I had known, often as an adversary, from my days on NDP council. I also had people like my friend Fred Penner on my show and lesser-known heroes like Oxford-educated lawyer

George Lockwood, who had moved to Winnipeg and then became counsel for Amnesty International Canada.

My connection with *City Magazine* also lasted for over twenty years. I went from reader to writer to associate editor to co-owner. It began as a political magazine out of Toronto, under the direction of James Lorimer in 1974, and quickly expanded to include architecture, city planning, art and other related topics. After a brief lapse, my friend Kent Gerecke, who was teaching City Planning at the University of Manitoba, picked it up. I was the Calgary correspondent at that time. I liked the format, which included city beat columns, articles, reviews, poetry and more. The product was good and we had some innovative marketing, working with a Canadian version of *Utne Reader* called BOAP (Best of Alternative Press) but advertising revenues were always a challenge.

When Kent died in 1992, Marcia Nozick picked up the leadership along with Robert Emeny and my friend Ross Dobson, who had been on CBC radio and television through the sixties and seventies. We renamed the magazine *New City*, after considering several alternatives, but the magazine never really got traction under the new ownership. It was a case of too few people, with too few hours and too little capital trying to do too much. Just because it was never a money-maker, does not mean it was not a success, but eventually the disappointment led me to resign with very harsh words in an exchange of letters late in 1996 and early in 1997. The magazine did not survive; fortunately, my friendship with Ross did.

Over the years, I interviewed many, was interviewed by many and generally enjoyed getting to meet and to know a whole host of people. David O'Brien, who wrote for the *Free Press,* is one of many that became a friend and I was always pleased to see him. He had a similar experience to mine with cancer and that always makes for a deeper connection. Wally Dennison, another good friend, was on the social affairs desk for the *Free Press* from 1972 to 1977. He is out in Victoria now but we keep in touch. He was very sympathetic to many of the causes and ideas I promoted. Glen MacKenzie lived in my co-op apartment back in the early seventies and then went on to a long career with the *Free Press*. He has retired, quite comfortably, in Thailand. Morley Walker is someone I have always enjoyed talking with about theatre and at times he was been one of people who reviewed my letters to the editor. Normally they call and

Community access TV: another platform for politics

make sure the person actually wrote the letter but I remember him telling me that they don't bother with me because "no one can impersonate Nick Ternette." There are some who I only met once or twice face to face but have had an interest in for years. Gordon Sinclair took it upon himself to trash me with misinformation when I was living in Calgary, and in Winnipeg, but wrote a lovely piece on me when I was sick. He was also a key supporter, if not the driving force, of the money-raising effort for Emily and me after my leg amputations.

Perhaps the interview I remember the most was with the recently deceased Christopher Hitchens. He was a Trotskyite who became a libertarian and is mostly known for his book *God Is Not Great*. The opportunity to interview him came through Peter Holle at an event where Hitchens spoke, sponsored by the Frontier Centre for Public Policy. I was surprised at how down to earth and friendly Hitchens was. It just isn't what you expect from an intellectual of his notoriety. He talked about admiring Milton Friedman, Joseph Schumpeter and George Orwell, while speaking quite poorly of Ayn Rand. Even if their take is different, I like talking to people that have read the same authors that I have. I don't hold to the strong atheist views he was so well known for, but his slogans such as "the market is smarter than religion" put his ideas in clear, concise and understandable language.

Nick at one of his many, many press conferences

I will debate and talk on television, radio and in newspapers anytime and anywhere. This is who I have become. Since Joe Zuken died in 1985, I was on the speed dial of the media for the voice of the far left. A lot of the left tell me they never listen to any of the commercial media. They say that they only go on the Internet and select their news sources very carefully. I am more interested in reaching the people who are not political but who read the paper and read my letters and like what I write. I often hear it makes them think in a new way. That's meaningful; it means my ideas have connected with another person and that may change them. That is what making a difference means to me and I will continue to do just that as long as my health lets me.

10

Legacy

"Knowing that people recognize my integrity and trust me to meet them as they are helps me cope with my impending death. I don't have to go around and try to clean up messes that I made."

My cancer has greatly compromised my immune system. This is what led to the flesh-eating disease that took my legs away. Any day I could find out my cancer is back and any day I could get an infection that could kill me very quickly. The presence of my own death has given me a new outlook on life. I can't help but think of my personal legacy. I have also been forced to think about end of life issues and produce an advanced care directive (known to some as a "living will") so that I have the best chance to die with dignity when the time comes.

On my fifty-seventh birthday, I had lunch with my friend Ray Torgrud. As we reminisced about the "old days," we discovered that we both have a fascination with our own mortality. Ray was seventy at the time and he died ten years later in 2010. We discovered in that conversation that we both read the obituaries every day and, even though there might be no one we know, we both had a seemingly "morbid" interest in them. We shared the fact that we had both attended many more funerals, due to the unexpected deaths of friends, in the previous years than either of us thought we would. We agreed that unexpected phone calls in the middle of the night instill an overwhelming fear in us that someone we know and love may have been taken from us by death.

I make mental notes of the parts of funerals that I like. I even keep the programs of funerals I attend. I hate the pictures of people in the obituary page. Half of them look dead — and they were taken when the person was still living! If I am to have a picture, I want one that shows me being active and alive. I like to think I am ready for my death but a number of years ago a total stranger contacted me because he liked my letters in the paper and wanted me to write his obituary for him. It took me forever to do it. I don't know why. I still don't know why. In the same way, when I was first diagnosed with cancer I said I would write my own obituary, but I only finished it in April 2012, several years later. I have also rewritten my will and started a charitable foundation to which my meager savings will go when Emily and I both pass on.

I have also left explicit instructions for my own funeral including the hiring of several local musicians to perform at the West End Cultural Centre. I remember my friend, Evelyn Ste. Croix, had her service at the West End in 2002 and had songs like "Singing for our Lives" by Holly Near and Ronnie Gilbert, "When I'm Gone" by Phil Ochs and Connie Caldor's "Bird on a Wing." Those are good choices! I have been to too many funerals in my life and I could never go to too many parties. I like parties and Emily throws a big one for my birthday every year. I also have a whole crew over for a dinner about a week or so before Christmas every year. Once a year, I spend the whole day cooking a goose and sharing it with friends. There is a common room in the residence where Emily and I live, and we fill it right up and have a feast, lots of conversation and usually live music. I like having my friends connect and get to know each other. Emily and I complement each other as hosts. It is hard work but work we consider well worth it. We had a party even in 2012, when I had to be brought home from the hospital and taken back once the party was over. I would not miss doing this for my friends.

There were over one hundred people at my fiftieth birthday. It was held at the West End Cultural Centre with all sorts of people taking jabs at me from the podium and great music by Karen Dana and Harry Havey. That was the biggest gathering, but we draw a good crowd every year. I want my funeral to be just like those parties.

As I sat at lunch that day with Ray, at what now seems to be a very young age of fifty-seven and in good health, I had lost all of my closest friends who should have continued to live with me and die with me. It was difficult to feel lonely at fifty-seven and spend so much time thinking about my friends who had died. I can no longer call them up and ask them to meet me for coffee. They live in memories. I still mull around in my head how and why they died so young, and why I am still alive. I went to the counselling centre at the University of Winnipeg to get some help and I just came to accept that one of the hard parts of aging is watching your friends die.

Willy Sheard died of lung cancer at the age of fifty-eight in January 2000.

Almost daily, he would call me and we would talk about personal things and share a coffee together. Willy was a reformed alcoholic who couldn't give up cigarettes. That's what finally killed him. Professor Kent Gerecke was my political mentor. Professor of City Planning at the University of Manitoba, Kent used to invite me to lecture on civic issues in his classes. Kent was also an active member of Alcoholics Anonymous and his program was his spiritual base. He survived a stroke at forty but died of diabetic shock at the age of fifty-two in 1992. Despite his ongoing illnesses, Kent never appeared to think about death. He was completely unprepared for it, and when he died, he left his estate in such a mess that it took more than two years to settle it. Werner Goetze was the third man I could call a best friend. He lived to age seventy but I was only fifty-five when he died in March 2000. He, too, had issues with alcohol. He lived the longest of my close friends, although he never did stop drinking until his very last days when his medical team had to prevent him.

Even though I have met thousands of people and worked with almost as many, I reserve the word "friend" for people with whom I can be truly intimate and vulnerable. I know I am a bit odd in this society and while I am thankful for the true friends that I have made, to lose my three closest friends before I was fifty-five made for a real hole in my life. It is strange to think that my three closest friends were alcoholics when I have only been drunk a handful of times. These aren't the only alcoholic friends I have had either. Maybe it wasn't so much that I was attracted to alcoholics as they were attracted to me. I treat everyone the same and maybe they were tired of being dismissed by others due to their drinking. These men were hardly copies of each other. Willy wasn't political and Werner was completely so. Willy was an extreme extrovert and friendly to all. Werner was sardonic and standoffish. Kent, as I said above, I knew for many years after he quit drinking and he was yet another person altogether.

I am a helper by nature, and in their own ways, maybe each of these good friends needed rescuing from time to time. Maybe it was just that my activity and order was like a break from their own inactivity and disorder. I'll be honest, I never thought about it in this way until it was pointed out by a friend helping me write this book. Whatever the reason, it is certainly a fact that I have been very close with a number of people with severe problems with alcohol.

My "fascination" with death, which began long before my illnesses, was only in part due to losing such close friends while I still thought of myself as young. It extends to dreaming about death and thinking about it in my waking hours. I have had a recurring dream all my life, less so now than when I was younger, of falling, which I understand is quite common. That dream is usually interpreted as fear of death and that makes sense to me. The feeling in these dreams was always that I absolutely needed to stop falling to avoid a huge, perhaps fatal, crash, but couldn't. Ironically, some people wouldn't hesitate to describe my entire waking life as some sort of crash.

I certainly don't have a sense of judgment like my mother had, in which she took her painful death as an act of God's anger and disgust with her. But, I do sense that we cannot help but evaluate our own life as we near the end of it. That is a part of my motivation in writing this memoir. I have left instructions for when I die to put a bullhorn and bright orange vest on a table at the front of the room where they celebrate my life. Those are the symbols of my life. I was a protester. I was a leader of protests. I like my nickname, Bullhorn Nick. I know who I have been.

In December 2012 and into January 2013, as I was waiting to hear back from publishers on this book, I was in and out of the Grace Hospital day by day for about seven weeks. I felt closer to death than I ever had. One night I was by myself in a hospital room and, thinking I was taking my last breath, I screamed in desperation. I was caught off guard. It made me realize just how much I don't want to die alone and in pain. I was sure I was going to die that night. When I started to feel a little better I spent a lot of time talking to Major Doris Jarvis, the Salvation Army chaplain at the Grace, who I had known since my cancer treatments. Major Doris was a comfort more for who she is than what she says. She is well traveled, well studied and no doubt has lots to say, but she is also just completely present, comfortable and open-minded. When she told me how I was one of the most spiritual people she had ever met, I was deeply comforted. No one had ever said anything like that to me before, and it is not a matter of pride. I was caught off guard, but as I wondered if each breath was my last, they were words I wanted to hear.

Emily also gave me a short but powerful book, *Mortality*, written by Christopher Hitchens as he was dying. The last chapter of the book is comprised of fragmentary notes that he was not able to bring together before his death. I thought his publisher honoured him by leaving them in that form.

I am not the rigid materialist or atheist that he was, but I found his words to be both overwhelming and comforting at the same time. His description of the experience of chemotherapy surpasses anything else I have read. His reflections on Nietzsche, in particular the phrase "that which does not kill us will make us stronger," helps put the constant immanence of my death in its proper context. In Hitchens' words, "I have decided to take whatever my disease can throw at me and stay combative … this is no more than what a healthy person has to do in slower motion." His description of that battle coming down, some days, to getting a few drops of blood out of swollen veins for testing is something I could not relate to more strongly. Like Hitchens, I face my death not convinced that I can or should take any pride or comfort in any strength that came to me through my illness.

Because of my name, St. Nicholas has always fascinated me. I have a wonderful doll of him I put out each Christmas and, in a small tribute to my Orthodox background, I have in my apartment a beautiful icon of him next to other mementos. As I lay awake at night in the hospital bed I found my mind wondering if my patron "Saint Nick" had wisdom to offer me. From my Orthodox background, I am sure, I have a strong sense that I have a soul that will survive. In fact, Abba Evagrius, one of the desert fathers, talked about our bodies becoming "dead and full of stench when the soul leaves." I don't spend time wondering about the afterlife or looking forward to anything it may contain, but this part of the faith — the existence of the soul — is important to me and I will be asking a representative of the Church to pray for the eternal comfort of my soul at my funeral. I trust in this as I confront the challenges I face. I guess this is faith.

When I had been so sick with my cancer and was actually clinically dead, I recall a vision of a glistening white Aboriginal man in a wheelchair coming towards me and backing away from me. One of my friends, Karen Toole, hospital chaplain at Health Sciences Centre, helped me see this as my spirit guide putting me at ease. Whatever it was, I know that my fear of death was greatly soothed by the vision.

The *Free Press* wrote an article about my "last speech to Winnipeg Council," which was arguing against the money being spent on police helicopters. I think that was fitting not because it pointed to anything in a precise way but for the exact opposite reason. It was fitting because I was simply addressing the issue of the day. I consistently brought a Marxist analysis to the issues of the day and saying crime prevention and a healthy community is a better way to spend money than fancy equipment to catch people after they commit crimes just makes sense. My last speech to council was "typical" and so it should have been. I probably spoke to council and its committees well over a hundred times in my life. I would see others there — lobbyists for the construction industry and Paul Moist, who would speak for CUPE at city council before he went on to becoming the national president. In fact, Paul and I often spoke from the same place on the same issues and would compare notes with each other. It was often clear that I was barely tolerated by some of the council, who would blink their eyes or close them altogether as if they were napping when I spoke. In contrast, Councillor Harvey Smith was always attentive and often asked questions or drew upon my suggestions in making his points.

The words "failure" and "success" are not really in my vocabulary. I am much more concerned about what I am doing than worried about how somebody else is evaluating what I am doing. Criticism bounces off me, leaving nothing behind. For all the abuse sent my way, the only time it had an impact was when Shawn Heron wrote real nasty stuff about me in the paper back in the early seventies. He used to refer to me as "The Ternette Man" — I can't even imagine what he was trying to say with that. Even then, it wasn't what he said about me that upset me, it was how angry my mother got. When I heard that she had sought him out to give him a piece of her mind I felt terrible that he had hurt her so much. If I let criticism bother me I never could have done what I did in my life. Even when Howard Pawley, when he was premier, called me a racist in the newspaper, I knew who I was and knew it said more about him than me. He knew ethnic politics had crept into the NDP and was undermining our historical roots but he had to play to the public. It was gratifying when he apologized, but if I needed an apology from everyone who spoke ill of me, I would have been very busy collecting them.

Obviously, I like the oft-quoted refrain, "If at first you don't succeed, try, try again." It is just that most people do not really follow it, even when they say they do. Of course, this assumes that the only way to succeed in an election, for example, is to get the most votes and win, but that is not my assumption. I am a Marxist. And I am in the less than one percent of Canadians who identify with the writings of Marx. I am not going to "win" at anything with that as a starting place and so, I try and try again. Maybe I'm putting myself down too much, but I really don't think that in forty years city council ever truly listened to me once. That does not mean that I haven't had an impact. I get e-mails and a lot of feedback from people who read about my fighting for bus fares and all the issues I have spoken out on, and they appreciate it. I seem to have had an impact on a wide range of average people: people who have little or no knowledge of how city hall functions, people who don't pay attention to politics in general, people who have given up on politics, people who appreciate the stances I took and the challenges I brought to those in power, people who felt I spoke for them because I was like them. I guess you call such things the (simple) "victories" of life.

Most people are surprised to know how much sports matter to me, and when I look back on my life I see sports are a big part of who I am. I wasn't a great athlete myself and was discouraged because of my accent to become an announcer, so I turned to coaching at a young age. I spent a lot more time on football fields than I ever did in protest marches in my life. I led practices four days a week and games on Saturdays. These were twelve-year-old boys practising four days a week from six to eight in the evening. I am deeply satisfied when I go somewhere like the Folk Festival and see this fifty-year-old Aboriginal guy screaming at me, "Hey Nick! Remember me?" Then he tells me what year I coached him and how football taught him about discipline and priorities and gave him life lessons that helped him stay out of trouble as he became an adult. None of the kids I coached played pro football or anything like that, not that I know of, but I have never met a single former player who has not made something productive out of their lives. I also had a long winning record as a hockey coach, which is really something when I think that I had never even put on a pair of skates before coming to Canada.

By any measure, I was a success at six-man football. My teams won the city championships three times. This was at the West End Memorial Community Club. Between hockey, football and baseball I coached well over two hundred kids over the years. When you read terrible stories of coaches who abused their players, it is important to remember the vast majority who poured years into coaching youth in sports and made a difference in many, many lives. Coaching is a part of my life that I am very proud of, knowing from many of these kids that their involvement in sport was a great part of their childhood. That means so much more than the wins and losses.

On top of the formal coaching, I also organized sports in other settings too. When I was working as an upgrading instructor in an Aboriginal education program at the old Osborne barracks, I coached all the team sports, on top of my regular work. We used a former residential school for our gymnasium space. I also helped the students form a student council so they could have a say in issues. This turned out to be important because this was in 1968 when several Czech immigrants fleeing the Soviet crackdown at the time actually displaced the Aboriginal students in the program. The Aboriginal program was moved all over the city into substandard buildings. This was my first more prolonged, more deeply engaged encounter with Aboriginal people. I was able to experience how they were treated in our society, regardless of which government was in power.

I always say coaching was a precursor to my political career. Political work, like football, is always done both collectively and competitively. I was competitive in sports and I am competitive in politics! I cut players as a coach. You had to cut players to put a properly sized team on the field, but if you were on my team, you played. I didn't play everyone exactly the same but if you were ready you played. I was also a coach who would stand up for referees. Often they were just young kids too and they didn't need to be pestered by the parents. I was a socialist coach, just in the way I did things and looked at the game.

I still love sports. Sports have taught me life lessons. Sports reflect all of the various social problems, psychological problems and political problems that exist in our society. The problems people have in knowing how to behave and how to treat their teammates and their opponents on the playing field are the same whether that field is athletic or political. My coaching skills helped me in terms of community organizing and coping with irrational behaviour and other problems. In a sense, every amateur sports team is, or should be, a cooperative. Learning how to make it work as a cooperative came in handy when I worked on political teams as well.

I was a bowler in high school, captain of a championship winning team in university, and bowled a 373 in five-pin in my late fifties. I loved playing golf even though I never broke one hundred in my life. People who don't know me personally usually drop their jaw when I tell them these things. I wonder what it says about political activism when you are not supposed to have a rounded life at all. Two teams that I cheer for are the Pittsburgh Steelers, who I have loved for years, and the Saskatchewan Roughriders. The first thing you see when you come into our place is a Rider hat hanging on a door knob. It is not as if I don't understand the tension about private ownership, collective ownership and money in pro sports. I don't buy into the idea that we need pro sports in order to develop good amateur programs, but that does not mean I can't appreciate the athleticism and competitive spirits of pro athletes. To be completely truthful, I just get completely caught up in the game. A friend said once that even when I had never had a drink, I could get as loud and boisterous as a drunk just from the excitement of watching a game. When the environment breaks down and collapses, will there still be people who are paid tens of millions of dollars a year to play sports? No. And that doesn't bother me in the least. It is the game and the competition that matters to me, not the business that has exploited the game. It doesn't matter whether you live in a socialist society or not, it's the same damn thing wherever you live: there are going to be winners and there are going to be losers. Sports are a great way to learn this and prepare for adulthood. When I was coaching, community clubs were the centre, the beehive of both sports and culture, and all that is lost. Clubs are only for the wealthy in the suburbs now and that is tragic. This is exactly the place where my interest and commitment to politics and my interest and commitment to sports meets. In going through my papers to submit them to the archives, I found a piece of paper, I have no idea where it came from, with the following written on it, titled "Code of Ethics for Coaches and Players":

For Players:
Play the game for the game's sake.
Be generous in winning.
Be gracious in losing.
Be fair at all times, no matter what the cost.
Be obedient to the rules.
Work for the good of the team.
Accept graciously the decision of the officials.
Believe in the honesty of your opponents.
Conduct yourself, at all times, with honour and dignity.
Recognize and applaud honestly and wholeheartedly the efforts of your
    teammates or opponents regardless of color, creed or race.

For Coaches:

The game is a game for happiness.

The rules of the game are to be regarded as mutual agreements, the spirit of the letter of which no one should try to evade or break.

Visiting teams and spectators are honoured guests.

No advantages are to be sought over others, except those of superior skill.

Officials and opponents are to be regarded and treated as honest in intention.

Decisions of officials, no matter how unfair they may seem, are to be accepted without outward appearance of vexation.

To win is always desirable. But to win, at any cost, defeats the purpose of the game.

Losing can be a triumph when the best has been given.

The greatest good to the greatest number is the ideal.

The Golden Rule in sport is to treat other persons as you, yourself, would like to be treated.

I have no idea where this came from; I certainly did not write it. I just had it in a file from coaching football in my twenties and I considered it worth keeping. A search on the Internet showed variations from everywhere, including a Charleswood youth soccer league, a rugby league in Miami and a beach lacrosse organization in Maryland. Interestingly, the Jeremy Benthem quote "The greatest good to the greatest number is the ideal" is left off most of the reprints. My point is, given room for interpretation, these lists are not a bad start for measuring my life, or any life.

While I have a bachelor's degree from University of Winnipeg, I am not an academic. I am not an intellectual. My writing and my speaking have been neither academic nor intellectual. I'm an activist and I did a lot of "shit work" that most people never do. You know, I got the police permits, I led the marches, I was the master of ceremonies, but I am not the one asked to be a major speaker in any demonstration. Like a football or hockey player, I knew where to fit in and I knew how to do what was needed and I did it without complaining.

There's a whole purpose of public demonstration. It isn't just to demonstrate, it's also to look good for the media and be taken seriously by the public. I do things without being paid, knowing I'll get by. I don't attach a sense of pride to being paid, although sometimes I regret that I have done so many things for free. Others, like some media people who are progressive, say, "No, you want me to do this, you have to pay me." I have friends who are freelance writers, and they don't do anything unless they are paid. But, that's how they make a living. For me, it's like a hobby.

On the other hand, feeling that people didn't always value me, I must admit, did get to me. People have interviewed me, picking my brain, and sometimes they barely say thanks. My friend Donald Benham once sent a group of students to talk to me for a paper they were writing. I spent three or four hours with them and they got an A+ on the paper. Some people are paid great money and are acknowledged for that kind of "consulting," and maybe if I had stood up for myself a little better, my life might have been a little easier. My choice was not to look for more money so that I never had to compromise, and while I have some doubts about that choice, I don't spend much time wondering how I could have done it differently.

I look at academics on the left I know, like Henry Heller, Cy Gonick, Jim Silver, Dan Chekki and others, and I know I could not have taken that path. They have done great work and have contributed great things but I am left wondering if you can be a revolutionary if you accept the capitalist system enough to take the benefits that being a working academic brings. I don't sneer as much as I did when I was a younger because most of them are friends of mine. I don't get mad and I'm not jealous but I don't have an answer when poor people who join the movement look and say, "These people are hypocrites. You can't live a middle-class lifestyle and be a revolutionary."

I don't know how revolutionary anyone can be in the advanced capitalist system that we have. It took a long time to get where I am; I didn't intentionally choose a career path. I started writing letters in 1971 once the media started to attack me, and all of a sudden I became known and the public loved the fight I had in me. I started to appear on Peter Warren's radio show regularly because I was not going to take being torn to pieces without fighting back.

They say you can't fight city hall. Well, I am living proof that you can. I have spent my life doing just that. Peter Warren once said to me, "Nick, you know, you're not afraid. We disagree on just about everything but every time I asked you to come on the show you would come and you answered what you saw as the truth." And people decided that they respected me as a result. It sounds so simple, but I know I stand out because most people don't do those simple things. Most people don't stand up for their beliefs. Most people spend their lives compromising and, in return, receive comfort and predictability. Most people spend way too much energy just making sure they are liked. The stakes were different for me and the stakes are still different for me. That is why I look and sound different than other people. Politically, I think I live on a different planet; I was certainly often treated that way. It was and is simply not my nature to take such reactions personally. I see the whole picture; my own little ego is dwarfed by the need for human evolution to go beyond capitalism.

Things that seem obvious to me seem like the ideas of a lunatic to others. That does not mean I am a lunatic. I have to keep that distinction clear. I have never tried to be something that I wasn't. That makes for good sleeping at night. That is why I could befriend libertarians, right-wing populists and other people with whom I couldn't possibly disagree more. I would be quite happy to go to their homes and meet their families or make a habit of having breakfast out with them. I know who I am and I can treat them with respect because I respect myself. Had I given in each time I met a compromise on my path, I wouldn't have that self respect and I would feel my shame in front of those that I oppose the most. I couldn't be me. What would happen if I constantly doubted my own compromises? That would be a hard life! A few years ago, the leader of the Liberal Party came to my birthday party. I don't have any use for anyone in the Liberal Party in Canada, but Jon Gerrard is a nice person. I spent my twenty-sixth birthday with Izzy Asper. He wasn't a Liberal. He was a libertarian. He came and I had a bunch of NDPers over and for the whole night he couldn't escape. We had twenty NDPers surrounding him in one corner of a room, tearing him to pieces. I don't know how he survived the party, but he stayed for four hours. I took that as a great sign of respect for me. He was a bit of a fighter too; he probably loved the challenge.

Bob Wilson, a former Conservative MLA, is a friend of mine. He still keeps in touch with me. Poor guy had so many turn their back on him when he was charged with drug offences, but he stayed connected to me. Knowing that people recognize my integrity and trust me to meet them as they are helps me cope with my impending death. I don't have to go around and try to clean up messes that I made. I know any messes I made in life were because I didn't know any better at the time. They weren't because I was looking out for myself at the expense of others. I had opponents who chose to act hatefully towards me. I didn't need to hate them back. Joe Borowski, Sid Green, Jim Maloway and others in the NDP were threatened by my constant pulling to the left. Of course they were threatened, but I never needed to wear their insecurity.

I have mentioned my daughter, Tegan, throughout this book. She had nine children, losing one to a miscarriage, one at childbirth and

This is who I am

another as an infant. So I have six grandchildren, some of whom I helped raise when we were in Wolseley together. Emily and I loved that time of our life. Emily had no children and my daughter spent most of her time growing up with her mother in Montreal. Being grandparents was an opportunity Emily and I had not really imagined and we were about as hands-on as you could be. Seeing a milestone like using a cup, taking a step or speaking a word was a new experience for both of us. Although we were often drained physically, it was as enriching for our souls as you could imagine.

Tegan, herself, was very bright as a child. She could play crazy eights at the age of one and a half. I remember her playing pool at the Indian and Métis Friendship Centre in Sioux Lookout when she was so little she had to be held up to see the table. She learned the layout of the town almost right away and would run ahead of her mother to the centre if she was late getting out the door. She was the head of the student union at John Abbot CEGEP in Montreal, where she studied dramatic arts, and was active in supporting labour rights and opposing war and apartheid. She lived in Winnipeg right after her graduation. I loved being around to support her raising her children in Wolseley before she moved back to Montreal. No one would call her bookish, but she is a very bright and intelligent woman.

When I got sick in December 2012, Bev must have got word to my daughter that I could be dying. Tegan phoned me. We had been estranged for more than six years. She had cut off all contact with both me and her mother, who lives not far from her in Montreal. Bev has the occasional indirect update to give me, but that is it. This is certainly not the way I wanted things to be and it broke my heart, but age has taught me to accept the things I cannot control. Tegan chose to cut off contact with both her parents and I had to respect her choice. She grew up with a mother and father who were at odds with the way the world is and no doubt that has left her struggling for her own identity as an adult. I need to respect that as well. When she phoned I was really too sick to have much of a conversation but she said, "You are my dad and I love you no matter what and your grandkids love you and miss you." I had neither the energy nor the time to explore further. I received her call and her words as a simple and beautiful gift. She told me a few things, like the fact that she, her husband and all the kids are living an Orthodox Jewish life, but the purpose of the call was clear. She loves me as her father — a wonderful moment of grace and love in the midst of a bout of illness that left me weak, retching and fearful.

I expect when others remember me, it will be for the many elections I entered. Elections were a good way to make a point because people were paying attention. You had debates, people would ask questions and they would listen. That is why I ran in twenty election campaigns. It is not complicated. Yet, no one else in our city of 700,000 has made that choice and I can live with the reality that some people say that makes me crazy. To me, it was a tactic and a strategy. I had a point to make with my life and I used whatever tactics and strategies I could. I am not complex.

My idle is set on high. I know that. My friend Peter Globensky once wrote that my "blood pressure was as high as the decibels [in my] speech." I am passionate. I care. I give a shit. Today, people who are overly active can often get a diagnosis like ADHD. These are not things to be ashamed of; this is just the way I am. My friend Floyd Williston suggested that my accent coupled with my intensity scared people and prevented them from hearing what I had to say. So it is with them, not me, that the problem lies. I've also heard comments about my messy hair, or that I wear clothes with spills or stains or that people are unnerved by my lack of eye contact. As I said earlier, these days people might want to label me as having Asperger's syndrome or say I am a "high functioning autistic," but what good is a label at my age? This simply doesn't interest me. I am disappointed when people don't see past my personality and don't listen to my ideas. When I have been called a moron, a crackpot or a wingnut (and believe me, I have heard them all!) it washes off me like water off a duck's back. But, it usually means they haven't listened to my ideas and have, therefore, not engaged with them; and the ideas, the analysis and revolution are important!

... and this is who I am

I see my life as being more about choice than obligation. I was committed to movements, not groups. I was committed to an ideology, not a political party. Therefore, there were times when I acted out of a sense of obligation to the movement or organization I was part of. More often, unlike those who spend their lives much more strongly identified with their job or office or organization, I constantly had choices to make rather than obligations to fulfill.

I was once called "Winnipeg's Rick Salutin," and while I admire him and take comparison to this Torontonian novelist, playwright and journalist as a compliment, I have no need for such praise. I am quite happy being Nick. That is my name. That is how I introduce myself and that is enough.

If I am going to call myself a "professional radical," a phrase Saul Alinsky used in his book, then I had better be prepared to actually do things and not just bark at others from the sidelines. Being a radical is being able to do the hard work of not only looking for the root causes of the inequities of our society but also being engaged in solutions. I am a man of service and a man of friendships, still. Our phone still rings, sometimes seemingly constantly, with people wanting my advice, help, direction or support with the problems that are keeping them from living a truly free life.

Some have said that I can be neither defined nor refined. This much I know. I am a Marxist. I am a new leftist. I am a libertarian socialist. I want a better life for all. I believe that caring community is a necessary part of being human. That is who I am.